Syria's Economy and the Transition Paradigm

St Andrews Papers on Contemporary Syria

SERIES EDITOR, RAYMOND HINNEBUSCH

Changing Regime Discourse and Reform in Syria
Aurora Sottimano and Kjetil Selvik

The State and the Political Economy of Reform in Syria
Raymond Hinnebusch and Soren Schmidt

Syria and the Euro-Mediterranean Relationship
Jörg Michael Dostal and Anja Zorob

Syria's Economy and the Transition Paradigm
Samer Abboud and Ferdinand Arslanian

Syria's Economy and the Transition Paradigm

Samer Abboud
Ferdinand Arslanian

University of St Andrews Centre for Syrian Studies

Published by the University of St Andrews Centre for Syrian Studies
School of International Relations
Fife, Scotland
UK

Distributed throughout the world by
Lynne Rienner Publishers, Inc.
1800 30th Street
Boulder, CO 80301
USA
www.rienner.com

British Library Cataloguing-in-Publication Data.
A catalogue record for this book is available from the British Library.

Printed and bound in the United States of America

ISBN: 978-0-9559687-0-9

Contents

Foreword

Raymond Hinnebusch

Syria is embarked on a transition from a state dominated to a market economy, but does the government have a road map? Samer Abboud suggests that transitions vary along a continuum from neo-liberal shock therapy with full scale privatization of the public sector to the Chinese model of marketization in which the public sector survives within a gradually activated market economy. Syrian policy makers have referred approvingly to the Chinese model which is compatable with the survival and adaptation of the authoritarian regime. Abboud explains why Syria's path is closer to this end of the continuum and outlines the regime's moves toward marketization through economic liberalization. Ferdinand Arslanian takes up the analysis with an empirical comparison of Syria with other ex-communist transition economies meant to locate Syria's tangent along the continuum, in terms of the relative extent of liberalization and the accompanying performance of the emergent market economy. He identifies substantial deviation from both ends of the continuum. These are explained by Syria's special features, alluded to by Abboud, notably hydrocarbons, a relatively low level of industrialization and high proportion of the economy in government, trade and other services, plus the persistence of a commercial oriented private sector.

1
The Transition Paradigm and the Case of Syria

Samer Abboud

Introduction

In June 2005, the Syrian Ba'ath Party held its 10th Party Conference amidst heightened US-French pressure over Syria's role in Lebanon and against the backdrop of a deteriorating economy. At the conclusion of the conference the Party put forth a series of recommendations on its regional and domestic strategies as well as the future direction of the economy. One of these recommendations commits Syria to a program of economic transition:

> Issuing the social market economy according to a gradual movement that protects the society, stressing the importance of the state's role in the economy according to modern models, and re-qualifying the public sector in the strategic sectors, and strengthening the participation of the private sector in economic activities.[1]

A series of policy and institutional shifts initiated since 2000 suggest that Syria has committed to initiating a structural transition away from a centrally planned to a market oriented economy. Much like Russia, Eastern Europe, and many countries in Asia, including China and Vietnam, Syria has initiated a transition away from traditional mechanisms of economic governance dominated by the public sector to increasingly marketized models of governance.

According to Yarbrough and Yarbrough (1997: 469), there are numerous countries, including over 30 in Africa alone that are currently in some stage of transition from central planning to a free market economy. Emerging from the experiences of these cases is a rich literature that has attempted to interpret, explain, predict and model the transition experience, a literature that will be referred to here as the Transition Paradigm.[2] In social science research the term 'transition' has typically been employed to signify processes associated with political and/or economic transformation. Despite the intersection of political and economic processes within these transformative circumstances, much literature – particularly within the context of Middle East Studies[3] -- remains tethered to a narrowly defined political transition. The hegemonic position in social science research afforded the study of political transition typically meant that the study of economic transition was relegated to the field of economics. However, in recent years the two strands of literature have begun to speak to each other, providing fertile ground for the study of the political economy of transition. When speaking of the Transition Paradigm, this paper is referring to this more contemporaneous strand of the Transition literature that emphasizes the multiple and interdependent geopolitical, social, cultural, ideational and institutional factors that produce and define transition within a country.

With this in mind, the aim of this paper is to ask two very simple questions. First, what can the Transition Paradigm tell us about Syria's economic transition? And second, what *can't* the Transition Paradigm tell us about Syria's economic transition? The question of how the Syrian transition can be understood in relation to the experiences of other countries must be framed both positively and negatively since the particular dynamics of the Syrian experience are not sufficiently captured by the empirical and theoretical work of the Transitologists. While we can draw on the framework of the Transition Paradigm to help us answer a number of important questions about the trajectory of Syria's economic transition, there are an equal number of questions that emerge out of the Syrian experience that are not sufficiently addressed by the paradigm.

Some prefatory notes on structure will prove helpful. First, a discussion of the concept of transition will be provided followed by a delineation of the various models and strategies of transition. The taxonomy of transition suggests that different strategies are motivated by the outcome of the marketization versus privatization debate. The distinction between the two strategies will be provided, demonstrating which 'model' Syria's transition clearly falls under. Third, the primary and secondary elements of transition will be identified and elaborated on within the context of Syrian policy. Primary elements are considered those factors that shape and direct the transition process, while the secondary elements are those specific areas of economic policy and practice that are undergoing change in the transition. As such, the majority of this section will focus on the secondary elements and Syria's various policy reforms in each of these areas. The paper will conclude with an assessment of the original thesis questions.

What is Transition?

Reflections on the political-economic trajectory of the twentieth century reveal a series of significant transitions, for example, from capitalism to socialism/communism. The collapse of the Soviet Union and the ascendance of neo-liberal economic policies throughout the world have reflected broader trends in the global political economy towards the hegemony of the market. Indeed, transition to free markets has even been heralded as constituting the 'end of history'. Despite the proliferation of transition economies in the last three decades, there is a key question yet to be sufficiently answered: what exactly is a transition economy?

The difficulty of establishing a definition of a transition economy is summarized by Papava (2005) who draws on a wide range of literature written in Russian. Papava defines the 'transitional period' as "a period of time during which a certain historical choice has to be made" (*Ibid*). Other approaches define 'transitional economy' as representing the negotiation between any two psychologically and theoretically opposed regulatory approaches. Institutionalist perspectives argue that the transition process is defined by the substitution, developing and functioning of formal and informal institutions, i.e. the market in place of the central plan. Finally, some definitions stress the inevitability of systemic transformation and locate transition economies within a broader context of interminable systemic adjustment. Definitional and terminological ambiguities notwithstanding, there are processes, policies, strategies and outcomes that are associated with economic transition.

The two dominant models of economic transition that provide the theoretical and conceptual tools for our understanding of the process have been the neoclassical and market socialist models.[4] The former is based on the transition process in Russia and Eastern Europe, both of which were defined by 'shock therapy' strategies, and the latter, commonly referred to as the 'gradualist' model, was employed in countries such as China, Vietnam, and Cuba. A number of strategies differentiate these two models. First, both are grounded in different expectations of the speed of the transition process. Shock therapy calls for immediate privatization over a period of a decade, while gradualism assumes that the transition process will take many decades. Second, shock therapy strategies prescribe that political and economic transition is interlinked and cannot occur independently of one another (*perestroika* and *glasnost*). The gradualist model, on the other hand, is premised on the belief that a country can undergo economic transition without corresponding political transition (*glasnost* with no *perestroika*). Third, in the shock therapy model the international financial institutions (IFIs) are strategically and financially embedded in the transition process, effectively defining it. Therefore, the transition process is exogenous. In the gradualist model, however, the transition process is endogenous, and there exists very little, if any, IFI participation. Finally, shock therapy calls for immediate privatization while gradualism argues for marketization, with each choice resulting in radically different reform policies. It is hypothesized that Syria approximates a gradualist transition to a social market economy.

Primary and Secondary Elements of Transition

The aim of the transition paradigm is to explain the process of establishing a market economy by looking at its constituent elements and examining what factors determine the nature of this process. This paradigm proposes that the transition process can be looked at with regards to primary and secondary elements. The model lays out elements that affect transition (primary) and elements that must be changed in this process (secondary), thus the paradigm is an expression of the causal relationship between these two sets of elements. The end goal is the establishment of a market economy but there is no fixed road for getting there; on the contrary, how this emerges is dependent on the interaction of the primary elements. The transition model tries to explain how the market economy emerges as the product of a new policy and institutional matrix.

The primary elements are those which shape and direct the transition process: speed; economic analysis; definition of a good society; political structure; ideological structure; initial conditions (existing economic conditions); and geopolitics. Transition is meant to initiate changes in the secondary elements, which are: price-liberalization/stabilization; restructuring and privatization; institutional structure; monetary policy and the financial system; fiscal policy; international trade and foreign aid; social policy; and the role of the state. The strategies, approaches and models of transition are determined by the ways in which primary elements impact the secondary elements. Thus, the aim of this analysis os to begin to answer what the Transition Paradigm can teach us about Syria's economic transition through an examination of the progress of Syrian economic reform in the secondary elements. The discussion of the primary elements below is intended to demonstrate how the Transition Paradigm conceptualizes each element within the context of market socialist transition.

Primary Elements of Economic Transition

Speed.

Speed is perhaps the most important primary element and varies according to whether international or indigenous institutions drive transition. This refers to the time period in which transition is to be initiated. Under the shock therapy model privatization is pursued vigorously and quickly within a period of around ten years while under the market socialist model marketization is pursued over decades of economic reform. The choice to pursue either privatization or marketization determines the model/approach adopted in transition economies. The former process refers to the transfer of income power to property users, while the latter refers to the transfer of control power to users. The goals of privatization are to link the rewards of property owners with the profit of an economic unit (Wu 1994: 19). Alternatively, the goal of marketization is to transform economic units from centrally planned units to autonomous units capable of making decisions on production and exchange in response to market principles, rather than central planning dictates. Both processes serve to fulfill two features lacking in centrally planned economies: privatization seeks to increase motivational efficiency while marketization seeks to increase allocative efficiency. As a reform strategy, privatization is associated with the selling-off of public sector assets, while marketization is associated with the gradual interaction of public sector enterprises in a market economy alongside private sector enterprises.

The strategic model of economic transition in Syria is underpinned by an elite and regime commitment to marketization. While briefly discussed earlier, marketization refers to a process in which the allocation of public sector resources become determined by markets, rather than by a centrally planned economy (Biesbrouck and Jackson, 1995). It also refers to the transformation of state-owned enterprises into market actors. Although this is a complex, interrelated process, it consists of four primary features: (1) market-oriented reform in the administration and management of state-owned property and firms; (2) diversification of state-owned enterprise assets; (3) the encouragement of market-oriented behaviour by state-owned enterprises; and (4) the formation of mechanisms to encourage state-owned enterprises to compete on open markets (see Wedeman, 2003). Other features of marketization include a reduction in subsidies to state-owned enterprises, price reforms and reshaping labour laws.

Economic analysis.
This primary element of the transition process refers to the ideological underpinnings of economic policy in the transition process. Under the market socialist model, economic analysis remains nominally tethered to socialist economic analysis. Since market socialist countries have remained relatively independent of IFI policy prescription, they have been able to generate economic reforms that are compatible with previous economic policies and institutions that had developed during decades of central planning. In other words, while these countries adopt economic liberalization measures, they attempt to maintain coherency with pre-transition policy. The political imperative of regime survival in countries such as Syria renders total abandonment of state control as politically unfeasible. Thus, in the market socialist model economic analysis remains tethered to sustaining political structures: regime maintenance as opposed to regime transformation. More specific economic analysis emerges in addressing macro- and micro-economic reforms.

Definition of a good society.
There are four elements (Marangos 2003) in defining a good society: the view of existing social reality; a view of what constitutes a good society or the desirable end state of transition; desired changes; and the means of initiating the desired changes. The first element refers to socio-economic structures produced by decades of central planning, and recognition of how these structures facilitated economic policy. This is important in determining what facets of the existing system are able to fulfill transition objectives and should thus be retained, and which features should be restructured or eliminated. The second element that refers to the vision of a desirable end state of transition suggests a vision for how society and economy should be structured after the transition process. A view of what is a 'good society' is designed to filter assessments of economic and non-economic activity in the transition process. The third element, desired changes, must be seen as compatible with the transition vision of a good society. Transition to a market economy does not simply require the articulation of a desirable end state but a means by which to achieve this state. Finally, the fourth element refers to the appropriate mechanisms employed to encourage the desired changes. These mechanisms must be compatible with the economic analysis underpinning the transition process. The Syrian government's definition of a good society is expressed through the guiding phrase of a 'social market economy': a vision that seeks to reconcile market-led growth with social harmony and security. Reflecting this concept and a

broad public and elite consensus on the necessity of a gradualist transition to a market economy, Abdel Nour (2001) has argued that the reform process is guided not by a drive towards modernization and privatization, but rather by the need to balance modernization and economic growth with the guarantee of social equity and welfare.

Political and ideological structure.[5]
Political structures play a critical role in determining the speed of reform (Desai 1994). Under the market socialist model, the imperative of regime maintenance dictates that the transition process will be gradual and long-term so as to maintain existing political structures. In contrast to shock therapy proponents who locate the firm as the most transformative actor in the transition process, the gradualist approach suggests that the state is the most transformative agent in the move towards marketization (Wilson, 2007: 251). In the former model, the firm becomes the most important actor because it makes demands on the state. In this view, economic policy emerges out of the bargaining process between capital and the state. This of course is premised on the idea of the existence of a democratic polity. In the absence of democratic participation, such as the case in Syria, the state assumes the role of the main transformative agent in the transition process.

In Syria, domestic debate over economic reform has been wide since 2000. In a *EuroMeSCo* paper, Ayman Abdel Nour (2001: 6) argues, "the impetus for reform arose from internal pressures and from elite awareness that this would be an essential step to confront rapid change in the wider world". At the same time, there is a broad consensus that reforms should be gradual and aimed at alleviating potential socio-economic hardships generated by them. As such, though prominent economists have debated Syria's options for transition, party officials, the business community and the general public have never realistically contemplated mass privatization as a strategy in Syria. Such a strategy is considered not only a recipe for certain economic collapse, but also acquiescence to the imperatives of the Washington Consensus. As in other market socialist transition countries, the rejection of mass privatization is recognition that shock therapy is not the most appropriate method to introduce a market economy (Kolodko, 1999).

Perthes (2001: 143) claims that, though reform has always been piecemeal and driven by the needs of the moment, Syrians have begun to enter into open and lively debates about the country's economic relations and the strategies needed to make transition to a market economy successful. An emerging trend within these debates emphasizes not simply the necessity of reform, but the strategies of reform as well. In his 2000 book *al-aslah al-iqtissadi fi Suriyah* (Economic Reform in Syria), Nabil Sukkar identified three models of economic development that Syria could follow. The first, the 'Asian Tigers' model, is criticized on the basis of its subservience to the speculation of foreign capital. The second, the 'Russian model', is rejected as a predominantly political, versus economic, model of development. Despite its flaws, Sukkar identifies the 'Chinese model' as an appropriate strategy of economic development for Syria.

Indeed, this model has won out in debates over economic reform in Syria.[6] There has been no serious recognizable elite contemplation of the shock therapy model. Perthes (2001: 149) has referred to Syrian reform strategies "system maintenance by reform," while Heydemann (1992) has demonstrated that Syria's 'selective' economic stabilization programs were primarily political measures aimed at strengthening the authoritarian regime. As such, rather than dissolve or take measures to weaken its power, the Ba'th Party has opted to follow the strategy of *organizational adaptation* adopted by the Chinese Communist Party (CCP). According to this strategy, the Party and its associated networks position themselves towards the goal of increasing economic productivity, growth and output such that they can profit from marketization. Shevchenko (2004) views the CCP's organizational adaptation as "entrepreneurial," given that there is rent-seeking and corruption yet party cadres accept a necessary degree of compliance with central policies.

The underlying principle of Syrian economic reform has been an approach developed in China; that of market socialism, in which the government introduced market mechanisms while retaining public ownership (Ye 1991). This is most clearly manifest in the language and discourse of a "social market economy" that saturates the most recent Five Year Plan (FYP). More importantly, however, is that the China model of marketization initiates economic liberalization in the absence of political liberalization, unlike the strategies pursued in the former Soviet Union and Eastern Europe which linked the two processes. This model thus provides an approach for the preservation of one-party political and economic hegemony, which is pursued by maintaining the public sector institutions that have been developed under one-party rule. Rather than dismantling these institutions, as is the case under the privatization strategy, the economy is expanded to allow for private sector activity and investment and the public sector is encouraged to compete on liberalized markets with the private sector. This 'liberalization at the margins' strategy (sometimes called dual-track liberalization) means that a market economy is introduced parallel to (rather than in replacement of) the existing centrally planned economy.

The initiation of the Syrian reform movement must thus be understood as a process that was decidedly state-led and reflected the conscious decisions of the Syrian leadership. Since states such as Syria have built their legitimacy on the decades of state-led planning prior to reform there can never be serious consideration of mass, large-scale overhauls of the economy. Nevertheless, the leaderships' decision to initiate economic reforms is grounded in recognition of the supposed utility of capitalist reforms to generate material wealth and economic growth within the economy. Since the Syrian leadership is unable to publicly embrace capitalism – a move that would surely discredit decades of state-led planning – they take refuge in the vague identification of Syria as a "social market economy." Whereas the state has sought to roll back many of the economic structures that were embedded in the central planning system, it has preserved key pillars of this system, including public sector enterprises and assets, avoiding their privatization. In this view, there exists mutual interdependence between the state and the market (Mizobata, 2007: 294) such that the survival or collapse of one directly affects that of the other. Thus, under gradualist models of transition authoritarian political structures are necessary to produce economic stability, growth and development.

However, the relationship between authoritarianism and gradualism can produce different economic paths and outcomes. That China serves as a model does not guarantee that Syria's future economic development will mirror China's in any significant way. For example, in China the public sector enterprises have demonstrated that they can be responsive to internal managerial and production reforms and hence compete on markets with the private sector. Policies such as decentralization and enterprise restructuring have also been successful in strengthening the overall capacities of the public sector. However, in Syria, current reforms have not been successful in generating public sector restructuring, despite efforts at reforming the banks and introducing new managerial systems. Quite simply, current reforms have not initiated any significant public sector restructuring. Thus, there is the very real possibility that economic reforms could generate the type of state-society-economy nexus that emerged in Egypt in the wake of economic reforms initiated in the 1990s, reforms which also failed to initiate substantial reforms of the public sector. Jordan also serves as an example of how authoritarian political structures were maintained and strengthened within the context of gradualist economic reform. There is also the possibility that Syrian economic planners could concentrate on attracting investment in services and tourism at the expense of establishing a productive industrial and manufacturing base, as has been the case in the United Arab Emirates, especially Dubai. This is an interesting prospect given the flow of petrodollars from the Gulf into these sectors in Syria. While China, Egypt, Jordan, Dubai and Syria are all unique cases in their own respects, they represent different strategies and outcomes of economic reform in authoritarian states.

Initial conditions.

Karshenas (2001: 60) points out that in the context of the Middle East and North Africa the underlying structures of the economies, arising from their resource endowments, past development experiences and external economic constraints, provides the context in which to understand gradualist reform in the region. Economists have tended to restrict their treatment of initial conditions under transition to the initial economic conditions (Heybey and Murrel 1999; Popov 2000). In addition to economic factors, including the three above points, it is necessary to have a more comprehensive picture inclusive of other variables such as social structures to have a more accurate understanding of the effects of initial conditions within a particular transition since these factors are all embedded in the economy (Bim, 1992: 181; McKinnon, 1995: 63). Consequently, the speed, sequencing and model of transition adopted in each country differs since they all initiate transition with different and uneven factor endowments (Kornai, 1999: 164; Herr and Westphal, 1991: 323).

One of the most important initial conditions is the initial source and control of wealth within a transition economy. The socio-economic landscape of a country sheds important insight into the question of rent-seeking within the transition context. This is particularly relevant in Syria's case as its political economy has been characterized by a reliance on oil rents since the 1970s. This would also suggest that the gradualist model aims to preserve or at least minimize the negative impacts of reform on rent seeking networks that have developed since this period. Other important factors include the existing level of industrial development; productive economic sectors; existing trade patterns and comparative advantages.

The most important initial condition in Syria is oil and the consequent shaping of state-society-economy relations that developed over decades of reliance on oil revenues. Amongst the phenomena that emerged under the oil period were rentierism and the lack of economic diversification in the economy. Oil rents also allowed the state to pursue significant public sector expansion, protection of domestic industries, and a complex subsidies program that supported local development. The range and depth of political-economic interests that were cemented under the umbrella of oil rents is thus an important initial condition in Syria's transition. Despite the presence of oil, the importance of other resources on initial conditions cannot be underestimated. Syria is a country endowed with other minerals such as phosphates and natural gas, which complement its oil reserves. The country also is relatively rich in agricultural land, although mismanagement, erratic rain falls and weather patterns, below-average yields and outdated cultivation techniques have plagued the sector. Syria is nevertheless a country which enjoys a high level of agricultural self-sufficiency, especially when compared with its neighbours. A final initial condition worth noting is the relatively low levels of industrialization in Syria as a percentage of GDP. Unlike other transition countries, Syria's service sector actually enjoys a larger percentage of GDP then the industrial sector.

Oil, agricultural self-sufficiency and low levels of industrialization are just some of the larger initial conditions which shape transition in Syria. Unemployment is also a major initial condition. With Syrian unemployment over 20% and high birth rates, there is a major challenge in incorporating these workers into the labour force. Furthermore, as unemployment increases, urbanization rates increase simultaneously placing demands on services in urban economies. Naturally, Syria's geopolitical context must be accounted for. During Syria's military-political presence in Lebanon thousands of Syrian labourers worked throughout Lebanon's economy, but in the aftermath of Syrian withdrawal many of these labourers returned to Syria, increasing unemployment figures and placing further demands on the economy. Also, the Syrian economy has had to absorb hundreds of thousands, if not millions, of Iraqi refugees fleeing the violence and occupation of their country. Finally, perhaps one of the most significant initial factors is the survival of a vibrant and creative Syrian private sector. Despite regime attempts since the 1960s to curtail its political and economic power, the Syrian private sector was never decimated or brought to ruin. Rather, the private sector, elements of which have been brought into the regime's fold and made beneficiaries of economic policy, can serve to facilitate the transition process. Furthermore, since a private sector exists and does not need to be created, this places less demands on the government to privatize public sector enterprises.

Geopolitics.
Economists have tended to narrowly understand the non-economic variables of transition as being an ideological shift towards democracy and the market. Yet, in geopolitical terms, transition often represents a shift in external markets, trading patterns and international relations. For example, the geopolitical change from a Soviet satellite to members of the European Union (EU) drastically shifted the political and economic environments in the Central and Eastern European countries that better allowed them to benefit from the post-Cold War order (Kolodko, 2001: 301). The shift towards the Western bloc and the prospects of EU membership were instrumental in lending legitimacy to the political and economic reforms experienced during transition.

Syria's geopolitical context is quite unique, with the most factor its conflict with Israel. Related, the Palestinian-Israeli "peace process", of which Syria has always played a role, has defined the regional geopolitical context particularly since the mid-1990s. This was disrupted by the US-led invasion and occupation of Iraq, Syria's neighbour. It can be said with relative ease that Syria's current geopolitical context is hostile and not favourable to rapid political or economic transformation in the country. In this sense there are multiple geopolitical contexts contributing to this. First, there is not only the US-led occupation of Iraq but also increased US threats towards Syria for its 'interference' in Lebanon and Iraq. The Bush Administration has passed sanctions against Syria and has been very vocal in its opposition to Syria's relations with Iran, Hamas and Hizballah. Furthermore, this Administration has supported Israeli military attacks against Syria's alleged nuclear power plant. A second context is that of the EU's rejection of the Euro-Mediterranean Partnership (EMP) agreement with Syria. Originally considered as a means to buffer against US threats, the Syrian leadership quickly came to see the EMP as a tool for the EU to pressure Syria and advance American demands on the country. Finally, an equally restricting/enabling context is Syria's sour relations with other Arab states, particularly those aligned with the US: Egypt, Jordan and Saudi Arabia. That said these relations have not prevented continued economic cooperation between these states. In fact, as will be discussed below, Syria is enjoying increasing trade with its Arab and non-Arab neighbours (Turkey and Iran).

Secondary Elements of Economic Transition

The secondary elements of transition are those areas in which we see the emergence of a policy and institutional matrix underpinning a market economy. In market socialist, gradualist transition countries, there are five measures that are associated with transition (Kumsaa and Jones, 1999: 198):

> price and trade liberalization and the acceptance of the private sector as the main engine of economic growth;
> market orientation of public enterprises and the encouragement of new private sector entries into the market;
> relaxation of state controls over the economy and microeconomic restructuring;
> stabilization of the economy and the enactment of liberal investment laws to encourage the inflow of foreign investment; and
> adoption of liberal agricultural policies to improve output.

With these five measures in mind, rather than focusing on the eight secondary elements individually, this section will concentrate on the most relevant elements that address the five measures noted above. What follows is a discussion of the types of reforms that occur under the market socialist model, with examples given of reforms initiated in Syria. This is in no way an exhaustive list of the reforms initiated in Syria; they do, however, offer a perspective on reforms in each issue area.

Price-Liberalization/Stabilization.

In the market socialist model, price liberalization is initially implemented 'at the margin' of the economy. China developed the dual-track liberalization model under which plan contracts between enterprises are preserved but frozen at existing levels and price liberalization is implemented for production taking place outside the planned contract. The argument behind this strategy of price liberalization was that it provided the means to liberalize policies without eliminating the existing rents of economic agents (Lau, Qian and Roland, 1997, 2000). By design, the system preserves the existing rents of economic agents under the planning system and thus shelters them from liberalization while creating new rents and new economic actors on the market track. Price liberalization is thus Pareto-improving[7] since it is achieved without creating losers. This dual-track system can also reduce the disorganization effect of price liberalization (Roland and Verdier, 1999).

Syria initiated substantive price liberalization measures in 2004. Prior to this, the pricing system was determined by the government through a collection of various Ministries, economic bodies and budgetary forces such as the Price Stabilization Fund (PSF) and other direct and indirect subsidies. The pricing system was intended to govern all aspects of imports, exports, production and consumption within the country. Commodities were divided into three categories – essential, basic and luxury – with prices established according to the importance of the product to the public. The basic premise of the policy was to discourage consumption and luxury spending and to encourage spending on essential and basic products, including food and clothing.

One pillar of the pricing system was the government's move to relate prices to public income. Increases in the costs of production and subsequent rises in prices were to be matched by corresponding rises in wages and salaries to maintain consumer purchasing power relative to prices. Another feature of the pricing system was the gradual harmonization of international and neighbouring country prices to more closely reflect domestic prices, a measure aimed at improving export capacity. Private sector enterprises were treated as public sector entities through mandatory compliance with government pricing policies. Expectedly, this lead to the rise of black market activity, tax evasion and price distortions since real prices were impossible to calculate. Another feature of the pre-reform pricing policy was that prices operated on a fixed system. That is, because of subsidies prices of essential and basic goods remained the same, meaning that shifts in production costs were not reflected in the price of a product. This encouraged a chronic sellers market whereby the objective of production was quantity and not value (Kornai, 1992).

The fixity of the pricing system, tax evasion and black market activity made determining prices impossible. As the pricing system weakened, its institutions such as the PSF proved incapable of fulfilling their intended functions as the gap between wages and prices, a key determinant of the success of the pricing system, rapidly increased. Between 1975 and 2000 the price of consumption goods increased approximately 7185% while minimum wages over the same period rose only 883% (Jamil, 2001). Between 1985 and 2000 average spending on food increased 544% while minimum wage only increased 342%, a 200% gap between wages and basic food prices (*Ibid*). Moreover, living expenses in 2000 were 300% higher than those of 1978 while purchasing power of minimum wage earners in 2001 was lower than in

1987. By 2001, 96% of *all* government salaries fell behind the average living standards and 68% of those salaries do not even cover average nourishment costs as defined by the United Nations (al-Khatib, 2001). The huge gap between wages and prices is the context in which price liberalization policy was implemented in Syria.

Syrian price liberalization, which has aimed to reduce distortions, has rested on four axes: introducing incentive mechanisms through expanding public sector autonomy; selective and gradual price liberalization; aligning prices to domestic supply and demand; and trade liberalization. On April 18th 2004 Decree #2908 was passed by the government, centralizing all pricing responsibilities within the Ministry of Economy and Trade and setting out a new approach to price policy. In the memorandum to #2908 the government acknowledged that while it was ceding price control to the private sector, it would remain active in directing market mechanisms. This has meant that current Syrian pricing policy is based on four tracks, or four price categories. The first track refers to essential goods and products that are essential to fulfilling the needs of citizens, such as breads and oil. Goods falling under this track will remain subsidized. Goods falling under the second track will be subject to a price ceiling: the government will not establish what price goods will be sold at, rather it will determine the maximum price at which a good can be sold. The third track establishes an independent pricing policy for public sector management. Any products falling outside the first two tracks can be priced according to managerial decisions. Finally, any products not falling in the first three categories are products whose prices are determined entirely by the market.

Despite—and in some respects because of--the liberalization measures, prices continued to skyrocket and increasingly many goods, even essential goods, were pushed out of the reach of purchase by ordinary Syrians. For instance, since 2004 the prices of average food products have increased more than 20%. The price of fuel rose as subsidies decreased, and the increased price of cement drove up real estate costs, which were already on the rise due to a number of other factors, such as the influx of Iraqi refugees. Problems prevalent under the pre-reform pricing system have remained. Tax evasion has meant that many factories remain unregistered and outside the regulatory control of economic policy. Black market activity creates disequilibrium within the economy through distorting prices at all four tracks. Finally, fluctuations in international prices (particularly of steel) and currency exchange fluctuation have all negatively impacted price liberalization policy in Syria.

Restructuring and Privatization.

In Syria, restructuring and privatization within the context of transition has meant the simultaneous development of the public, mixed and private sectors (Polling, 1998). In the market socialist model, restructuring and privatization is expansive since it aims at creating new market opportunities for existing and new actors, while under shock therapy it is contractive because it transfers public assets to the private sector. Syria's economic restructuring and the re-balancing of the public-private axis is an endogenous process of reform that is driven by domestic forces rather than international actors.

Steps towards private sector restructuring include bringing the private sector into trade negotiations and expanding the opportunities for associational activity (previously banned). There have also been liberalizations of investment laws and the abolition of Economic Security Courts (Decree #16, February 15 2004) that were seen as a major obstacle to investment. Relaxations on foreign exchange measures were also meant to stimulate private sector activity and investment and increase export capacity. In 2002, the government abolished the exclusive import rights of state import agencies, meaning that the domestic private sector could now import directly from international traders. Also, in 2005, the Commercial Bank of Syria announced measures to ease lending to domestic investors. These multiple reforms aimed at expanding the capacities of the domestic private sector but they did not involve the transfer of public assets to the private sector. Generally, the Syrian private sector has not responded warmly to the idea of investing in the public sector. Thus, policy aims at both expanding the opportunities for private sector activity while targeting the public sector for restructuring.

In 2004, Law #51 allowed public sector establishments to enter into foreign contracts. The new law establishes how public sector establishments can secure their capital and labour needs and sell their assets, both domestically and abroad. It was passed to coincide with the implementation of the Greater Arab Free Trade Area (GAFTA) on January 1 2005. The law was meant to streamline and simplify the contracts system since the previous system was seen as a major impediment to the public sector's regional competitiveness and efficiency. Another important 2004 decision was to halt expansion of the public sector. This decision was made in conjunction with a move towards transferring management control of public sector enterprises to private contractors. Under this move, the public sector would retain ownership while the private sector would manage the enterprises. Finally, the government authorized private investment in joint ventures with the public sector, a move intended to attract the necessary capital to transform stagnant enterprises into competitive economic actors. The Syrian Arab Electronics Industries Company (Syronics) and the General Organization of Tobacco (GOT) have already entered into investment agreements with international firms. All these measures aim at gradually rehabilitating the public sector and attracting private capital to increase Syria's production and export capacities.

Institutional Structure.

Rodrik and Subramanian (2003) identify four types of institutions that compose the institutional structure of a market system. First, market-creating institutions are those that are concerned with the protection of property rights and the enforcement of economic contracts. The market would either not exist or function poorly in their absence. Second, market-regulating institutions are those that correct market imbalances and deal with market externalities. Third, market-stabilizing institutions deal with macroeconomic stability, ensuring institutional control over inflation, financial crises and market fluctuations. Finally, market-legitimizing institutions are concerned with the provision of social welfare and protection and are often involved in patterns of economic distribution.

Since Syria has not undergone mass privatization, there has not been significant institutional overhaul, especially of the fourth type. However, one of the most important measures has been the consolidation of decision making power within existing institutions. In 2004, along with substantial price liberalization measures, the government centralized pricing policy within the Ministry of Economy and Trade. Prior to this, pricing policy was guided by a committee consisting of representatives of the Economic Committee, the Ministry of Supply and the Executive Bureaus in the Syrian Governorates. There have also been significant centralization measures within Ministries, most notably the Ministry of Supply and Internal Trade. Many of its ministerial bodies were amalgamated, the rationale being to increase management, administrative and economic capacities of the Ministry as a whole. This general pattern of restructuring through amalgamation and centralization of responsibilities has characterized much of Syria's institutional restructuring under reform. While many of the institutions may not have changed, their responsibilities, capacities and inter-relationships have been re-shaped by reforms.

The most relevant new institution has been the revival of the Credit and Monetary Council (CMC), a body entrusted with the formulation and implementation of monetary policy. In practice, the CMC will act as the Board of Directors for the Syrian Central Bank[8] and, as stated in Article 1 of the Law creating the Council, its objectives will be to: 1) develop the monetary and financial market according to national economic needs, 2) maintain the purchasing power of the Syrian currency, 3) stabilize the foreign exchange rate of the Syrian Pound and secure its free exchange to other currencies and 4) work towards the growth of national income.

Monetary Policy and the Financial System.
The creation of the CMC can be seen as a response to the demands of monetary policy, mainly to create and maintain budget constraints and set monetary policy. This is achieved through reform of the banking sector, dividing its functions between a Central Bank and a number of commercial banks. In the market socialist model, a wholly private financial sector is discouraged. Reducing the potential power of private capital is important to ensure that the state has maximum control over the money supply and can thus assume responsibility for avoiding inflation. Under this model there exists a state-controlled Central Bank and a series of state-owned commercial banks, but there is also room for the introduction of private banking into the transition process, as long as these banks do not interfere with the stabilizing and distributive functions of the public sector banks.

There is no shortage of negative characterizations of the Syrian financial services sector that define the sector as underdeveloped, both institutionally and structurally, and incapable of responding to the demands of improving financial intermediation in the country. The State Planning Commission[9], for example, lists the following characteristics of the Syrian financial services sector: In spite of existing foreign currency controls, approximately 80% of imports were transacted through unlicensed currency exchange dealers. (High) interest rates were disconnected from inflation or exchange rates. Structurally, the public banking sector exhibited a high percentage of demand deposits compared to total deposits and a high percentage of unclassified debts. A high proportion of bank credits were given to the public sector and government deficit financing through loans from the public banks created pressures on the financial resources available for the private sector.

According to most observers of Syria's banking system (see Sader, 2001; Shahlawi, 2001; Shallah, 2001; Abu-Ismail, 2004; Sukkar, 2004; Aita and Seifan, 2005), there is clearly a need for reform. However there were differences over how reform should proceed (Sukkar, 2004). The debate over reform has been accurately summarized by Shallah

(2001), who identified three schools of thought. The first school considers public banks as important economic devices to administer the national budget, to direct the overall economy and to finance economic development (al-Zaim, 2001). This school believes that the banks are not in need of overhaul, but rather in being given special support to be able to avoid financial crisis and assist in economic growth. The second school adopts a much more critical perspective of the banks in Syria and argues that the banking system has failed in its roles and duties in the national economy and thus should be radically reformed. The third school calls for the development of public sector banking operations while simultaneously introducing private banks to operate alongside the public sector banking system (Sukkar, 2004). In other words, a private banking system should be introduced but not at the expense of the public banking system, which would be supported through necessary institutional and structural reforms. This third school of thought is the dominant approach to banking reform in Syria and reflects the dual-track liberalization of the overall banking system.

Dual-track liberalization combines several features. Public sector banks continue to play a dominant role in the economy and in banking services and would not simply be marginalized by the introduction of private banks. The official approach dismissed the idea of the privatization of public banks and reasserted their importance in national economic development. Hence, reforms would not deprive the public sector banks of existing activities or set the public and private banks against one another as rivals (Sukkar, 2004). Indeed, the existing reserve strength of the public sector banks and the initially low capitalization of private banks is a situation more conducive to cooperation than competition. Moreover, all public sector institutions are required to continue to conduct operations with the public sector banks, including deposits and financing. Although there is still no strategic plan for the restructuring of the public sector banks (Sukkar, 2004), they were to be supported through the introduction of new technologies and accounting systems.

However, the structure of the state banking system is simply incapable of fulfilling the financial demands of the transition to a market based economy. Realizing this, the government introduced private banks into Syria as the cornerstone of its broader economic reform program. Since 2001, there have been a number of laws and decrees that have served as the pillars of Syria's financial reforms. The most important of these include (Horani, 2004):

Law No. 28, April 26th, 2001 permitting the operation of private banks.

Law No. 29, April 26th, 2001, The Bank Secrecy Law.

Law No. 23, March 17th, 2002, which revived the dormant Credit and Monetary Council, and which gave the authority for the Council to specify interest rates and bank deposits, as well as to monitor the operation of all banks in the country.

Decree No. 59, September 9th, 2003 to combat money laundering.

Law No. 24 and 25 (2003) aimed at balancing the taxation system and strengthening tax collection.

Ministry of Economy and Trade decision No. 431, December 6th, 2002, which sets aside 500 million USD annually to pay for raw materials and imports for production.

Decisions by the Credit and Monetary Council No. 4 (May 28th, 2003), No. 39 (December 3rd, 2003) and No. 43 (January 25th, 2004) which all relate to lowering interest rates

Decree No. 33 (2004) which cancelled decrees 6 and 24 that had outlawed dealing in foreign currencies.

These reforms address a series of important elements of a market monetary system. First, they restructure the entire public banking sector and introduce private banking into the economy. Interest rate reform, which was needed after more than twenty years of Syria's banks operating with unchanged interest rates, aimed at introducing new mechanisms to increase competition between the banks and to attract local capital into them. The revival of the CMC also served to introduce new institutions responsible for overseeing the monetary system and for implementing monetary policy.

The most significant of these reforms from the perspective of a transition economy is the introduction of private banking. Thus far the record of private banking in Syria is difficult to construct given that these banks have only operated since 2003. Nevertheless, there are certain trends that offer some perspective on what these reforms have meant to the overall monetary system. First, since 2003 there has been a steady increase in the private banking sector's total assets, while the public sector has witnessed a decline in its assets. Deposits in private banks have also steadily increased since this period, while public sector banking deposits have decreased, suggesting that Syrians are transferring their money to the private banks. There has thus been a healthy yearly increase in the private banks' market share although this trend should be viewed with some caution as only a minimal percentage of deposits (less than 5%) are actually transferred to long-term savings accounts. Third, both the public and private sector banks have increased their credit lending. The positive, upward trends for the private sector banks can be expected given that they have only recently established operations. A host of other reforms remain necessary, either to formulate or implement, to expand the services and capacities of both the public and private banking sectors, and thus to strengthen the monetary system as a whole. Thus, while the initial outcomes of the reforms seem positive, the contributions of the private sector banks to the economy as a whole remains limited, their services restricted and their standards remain below international and even regional banking standards.

Fiscal Policy.

Under market socialist transition, fiscal policy is expansionary. Public investment/spending are key fiscal measures used by the government under market socialist transition to increase living standards and maintain public services and benefits; tax policy and structure are the most important determinants of fiscal policy. In Syria, the shift in fiscal policy from deflationary to expansionary began in the 1990s to compensate for the lack of investment flowing into the country. In more recent years it has been complemented by other trends such as the reduction of interest rates and the easing of credit access.

However, by 2003, despite access to substantial oil revenues, public spending in Syria was approximately \$300 USD/person, while neighbouring countries' (oil and non-oil economies) figures reached approximately \$1000 USD/person (Nejmeh, 2003). The potential for government extraction of revenues to support growth-stimulating public spending and investment in Syria is hampered by a series of existing phenomenon. First, national revenue distribution through wages and salaries is simply insufficient to fulfill growth needs. Jamil (2004) estimated that salaries need to be at least three times the level they are at now to contribute meaningfully to economic growth, hence tax revenues. Unemployment, which is currently at approximately 20% has a similar effect. Third, the returns on public investment, estimated at approximately 20%, are very low. A fourth concern is that the current overall budget is prepared by the Ministry of Finance while the Investment budget is prepared by the Planning Commission, with a resulting disjuncture between national spending and investment objectives. Finally, the state no longer has the resources to shoulder the burden of public investment and must thus rely on private investment activity to generate economic growth.

The government has long channeled oil revenues as substitutes for an efficient and functioning tax system. With the decline of oil revenues, however, the priority has become improved revenue generating mechanisms. However, the country suffers from weaknesses in tax administration. To claim that tax evasion in Syria has caused structural deficiencies in tax administration or that it has reached disturbing proportions in scope would both be understatements. Syrian economist Samir Seifan (2001) has outlined a series of tax evasion practices occurring throughout the economy. Simple measures of non-declaration or hiding economic activity are perhaps the most economically destructive measures as Seifan claims that more than 70% of *all* economic activity is hidden. Foreign enterprises not declaring income account for an estimated 4 billion SYP in lost taxes each year. There are also tens of thousands of small businesses and workshops that operate without licenses and permits, thus falling outside the taxation system. Additionally, there is significant tax evasion, which occurs not simply through avoidance but through active bribery and corruption of state officials.[10] Given these varied evasion measures, Seifan (2001) estimates that private sector tax evasion equals 50 billion SYP annually, a figure that does not accurately account for the significant black market activity in the country. There is a myriad of distortive economic effects of pervasive tax evasion, including strains on state revenues, increasing indirect taxes, strains on public investment spending, the spreading of corruption practices, and uneven competition between public and private sector companies. Aside from the structural distortions produced by oil revenues and the pervasiveness of corruption, there are a series of other targets of tax reform, including: antiquated legislation; contradictory legislation; and a lack of tax benefits and legislative ambiguities (al-Hussein, 2004).

Since 2004, the government has initiated a series of tax reforms aimed at addressing these deficiencies. For example, decree No. 61 (2004) abolished twelve consumption taxes on several products and services and imposes a set of streamlined taxes in order to end double taxation of industry and to give a boost to the manufacturing industry and to exports. Most significantly, however, were two laws passed in 2003 which were indicative of the tension between the state's distributive and extractive roles. Law No. 24 (2003) significantly reduced income tax rates and schedules on individuals and companies and is seen as part of the state's strategy to encourage the payment of taxes and to increase the purchasing power of Syrians. Its counterpart, Law No. 25 (2003), significantly increased penalties for tax evasion, including fines and possible prison sentences.

The two laws – 61 and 24/25 – reflect the general government approach to tax reform, which is based on three foundational axes: reducing taxes on resources of income in order to stimulate production and investment; counterbalancing this reduction by taxing income uses; and, finally, reducing taxes on consumption spending to generate consumer spending. On the first two axes, a series of decrees and laws have been passed to reduce taxation of income sources and to help generate investment and spending. Legislative decree #18 passed on February 14, 2004 and cancelled both Law No. 794 (in place since 1928) and Law No. 54 (in place since 1979) and abolished livestock taxes, instead replacing the tax with a general export fee of 100 SYP per head. In November 2003, Law No. 22 was passed and resulted in the capitalization of loans for the general debt fund, a move intended to stimulate borrowing. The third axis of tax reform intended to generate consumer spending has been characterized by the following measures passed through a series of decrees: cancelling fees on televisions, radios, alcohol and cement; relaxing controls on the distribution of sugar and salt; and cancelling agricultural production taxes (al-Hussein, 2004). At the time of writing, a series of other important measures were being formulated or considered by the Ministry under a 'financial reform plan' intended to completely overhaul the tax system and the financial sector, including reform of machinery tax legislation and real-estate related taxes, especially relating to foreign ownership.

Finally, in addition to these various reforms of the tax administration, the government has embarked on a major step towards increasing the revenue base through the promised introduction of a Value Added Tax (VAT) of 10% by 2009. The VAT will serve as a goods and services tax and will not apply to basic food products. In announcing the decision, Finance Minister Mohammed al-Hussein acknowledged that oil revenues were only expected to constitute 20% of state income and thus measures had to be taken to substitute for the dramatic loss of oil revenues which was around 70% of total state income in 2000. The introduction of the VAT is a measure aimed at both improving tax collection and increasing state income, although its introduction is likely in response to some of the failure of existing reforms to increase revenues through tax collection.

International Trade.

International trade is one of the key secondary elements of the transition process and a major determinant of structural change in transition economies. The liberalization of foreign trade is essential to the transition process (Sutela, 1992: 85), often forming the cornerstone of any transition strategy. As Tisdell (2001: 577) argues, former centrally planned economies are confronted with two dimensions of market forces, the creation of internal markets and the opening of national economies to the market forces of the outside world. Trade in market socialist transition countries poses a dual-reform dilemma. On the one hand, there needs to be reform of internal production practices to create regional and international trading partners and, on the other hand, there is the impact of international competition on internal reform. The interaction between domestic and international processes impacting trade in transition countries shapes the process in multiple ways. Thus, under the market socialist model there is a constant tension between the legacies of protectionism and the need for greater market expansion and trade to generate foreign currency and enhance enterprise competitiveness. Trade is typically conducted on a bilateral basis in the first periods of reform and in conjunction with the creation of trade incentives, such as credit facilities and eliminating any barriers to import/export that existed prior to reform. Since under the central planning ISI model enterprises were typically shielded from competition, market socialist transition must gradually support the restructuring of enterprises to compete on domestic and regional markets. Trade liberalization under the market socialist model thus functions as a 'building block' towards greater, more integrated regional and international trade.

In this vein, Syria has entered into a number of bilateral agreements with neighbouring countries such as Jordan, Iraq, Turkey, Iran and Saudi Arabia, in addition to its multilateral commitments, the Euro-Mediterranean Partnership (EMP) and the GAFTA. Many observers of Syria's economy confirm the importance of bilateral trade agreements in facilitating Syria's ascension into both the EMP and GAFTA (Qalla, 2005; Suleiman, 2005; al-Amadi, 2003), claiming that Syria's negotiation and fulfillment of the requirements of bilateral agreements will better prepare the economy for broader regional competition, facilitate the passage of necessary economic laws, decrease public sector monopolies, encourage private sector activity and attract investment. Bilateralism is especially important in the context of the GAFTA, since trade agreements with Iraq, Saudi Arabia and Lebanon all conformed to GAFTA provisions. This helped prepare domestic Syrian producers for regional competition prior to the opening of Syrian markets to other Arab companies.

Although GAFTA represents an 'open regionalism' model, it is by far the most advanced project of Arab economic cooperation in modern times. The GAFTA forced Syria to remove its tariffs and address its many non-tariff barriers. Khoury (2002) has noted that the most important aspect of GAFTA is in exposing Syrian producers to regional competition after decades of protection under central planning. Increased Arab cooperation also holds the possibility for expanded regional growth and development accelerated by inter-regional trade and investment. For example, as a member of the new Arab trading bloc, Syria will be more attractive for investors, as we see in the case of investors from China, Russia and Korea, whose substantial investments in Syria are stimulating production and export trade from within Syria's borders. Another feature of the GAFTA is that Syria's trade with Arab countries is in non-oil products; hence GAFTA can enlarge markets for Syrian industry and support the upgrading of production practices and the increase of value added in Syrian production.

These features of the GAFTA contrast sharply with those of the EMP. First, Syria's trade with Europe is heavily dominated by oil products such that any liberalization of trade between the EU and Syria would put Syrian producers at a severe disadvantage. Second, the EMP, unlike the GAFTA, financially supports Syrian infrastructural, institutional and policy development through various financial schemes. Institutions such as the Syrian-European Business Center (SEBC) or the ISMF are entirely funded by the EU. These institutions are active in supporting Syria's transition through research and publication of relevant economy and sectoral reports. More importantly, however, they support the creation of linkages between EU and Syrian traders, they support Syrian exporters in gaining knowledge of exporting practices and standards, they contribute to government restructuring of key Ministries and economic institutions and they offer financial support to small businesses wishing to export products to the EU. Institutional development, support and financing in any capacity is entirely absent from the GAFTA provisions. The 'open regionalism' model of GAFTA contrasts sharply with the functionalist model promoted by the EU, which stresses the development of institutions, institutional capacities and institutional modernization. Thus, while the EMP does not carry with it tangible trade benefits, the EU supports administrative and institutional reform in Syria, aids in the introduction of new technologies and practices into various Ministries and institutions, and provides relevant information on the domestic, EU and world economy, facilitating trade between Syria and the EU.

Conclusion

The Transition Paradigm helps us understand the emergence of a policy and institutional matrix in Syria that underpins the emerging market economy. Since Syria has not followed a transition that is grounded in theoretically-derived policies, specifically the prescriptions of neo-liberalism, but is a more pragmatic, even ad-hoc respond to its special conditions, the Transition Paradigm helps us understand the logic behind the government's approach to economic reform and transition. It can thus help us answer questions such as: why has the reform process been so slow? Do certain policies, seemingly inconsistent in the perspective of conventional economics, have their own logic? What the Transition Paradigm tells us is that the transition process in Syria will be, by definition, slow and disjointed, strong in some areas and weak in others, simultaneously economically painful and painless, and of course, long. Ultimately, the Transition Paradigm can help us think about why policies and institutions are erected, and how these matrices create and sustain or obstruct a market economy.

Yet, while the Transition Paradigm can answer important questions regarding the nature, scope and rationale of reform and the policy-institutional matrix of a market economy, there are a number of issues that the Paradigm ignores that must be included in any understanding of the process of economic transition in Syria. The Paradigm is rather state-centric in its approach as it sees the state as the transformative agent within the transition process. Thus, our understanding of transition must look beyond merely the state as a unit of analysis to help explain and interpret the transition process.

In the late 1990s a growing literature on the 'Varieties of Capitalism' (Hall and Soskice 2001; Amable 2003) emerged that sought to account for the trajectory of different versions of capitalism in advanced economies and other transition economies throughout the world. The approach is actor-centered and sees the domestic political-economy landscape as populated by multiple and pluralistic actors. These actors include individuals, firms, government officials, networks and producers/industrialists. In this literature, actors interact with each other through various institutional modes, they are the key agents of adjustment and it is their activities that determine the different levels of economic performance and growth. This approach helps us overcome the state-centric logic of the Transition Paradigm that concentrates on the state as the transformative agent in the transition process. This literature begins to tell us about what the future of transition in Syria may look like, how a market economy may or may not develop, and what long-term challenges Syria faces. Most importantly, this literature tells us about how non-state as well as state actors operate within the policy and institutional matrix of a market economy, something which the Transition Paradigm generally ignores.

This ultimately is a question of governance that the Paradigm overlooks. While it can help us understand the emergence of a market economy through the creation of policy and institutions, it is less useful in helping us understand how economic actors operate within, and indeed outside, this matrix, and in turn what impact this has on the prospects of transition to a market economy. Simply put, economic reforms will be ineffective if economic actors do not mobilize within the emerging matrix to make the reforms successful and durable. The act of establishing capitalist legal structures does not guarantee their operation according to market precepts. For example, Syria has witnessed a significant spike in foreign investment in recent years but this has not been the result of liberalized investment or trade laws. Rather, increased investment has primarily flowed from the Gulf countries which are enjoying excess liquidity in the wake of the boom in oil prices and investing heavily in the services and tourism sectors. There is not much evidence to suggest that reform measures have actually initiated large-scale productive investment in industry and agriculture.

Furthermore, the role of class is ignored in the Paradigm. Linda Fuller has noted that in the transition literature, the previous 'mass' has been superseded by an equally homogeneous 'public' or 'citizens'. This homogenizing language serves to alienate any class analysis from the discussion of transition economies, especially in the market socialist context that views the state as the transformative agent in the transition process. However, in the transition period, Lane (2005: 421) has argued that the rise of classes is stimulated by marketization and the replacement of administratively determined incomes by market-oriented ones. A class analysis of transition can thus help explain the forces underlying the tug of war in the transition process, and it can help us better understand the processes of economic dislocation and marginalization that are revealed in the context of transition. Again, the Transition Paradigm ignores the potentially transformative role of class within the context of economic transition. Growing class inequalities in Syria generated by inflationary and price fluctuations, high unemployment, wage stagnation and increasing costs of living, mean that class issues will shape the future trajectory of the domestic political economy as it undergoes transition.

Nevertheless, the Paradigm offers a wealth of theoretical and conceptual tools from which to understand the process of economic transition in Syria. This paper has attempted to introduce these tools and in doing so has established a broad approach to help encourage understanding, debate and negotiation of the process of transition in Syria. Drawing on the experiences of transition countries throughout Europe, Asia, Africa and Latin America, the Paradigm can not only help us understand the specificities of Syria's transition, but it also allows us to view Syria's transition comparatively.

---

[1] Ba'th Party recommendations published in *Al-Ba'ath* newspaper, June 13 2005.

[2] Others have used the term 'transitology' to refer to the study of transitions.

[3] See Brownlee (2005: 45-48) and Perthes, Volker (ed.) (2004) *Arab Elites: Negotiating the Politics of Change.*

[4] A third strategy, associated with the transition process in the Balkans, is referred to as the 'Third Road,' or 'Gradual Gradualism,' which refers to market transition as a long, tedious process, where privatization is restricted to small enterprises, and private ownership is permitted only in trade, services and tourism (Berend, 1995: 133-137)

[5] Considering that political and ideological structures are interconnected elements, to avoid repetition the discussion of the two elements has been merged.

[6] See several documents prepared by the State Planning Commission in both English and Arabic. The most relevant in demonstrating the Syrian commitment to dual-track liberalization are *Highlights of the Syrian Economy and the Tenth 5YP Strategy* (2006), *The Management of Economic Planning in Syria* (2006), and *The Framework for Financial Sector Reform in Syria* (2006). See all the Institutional and Sector Modernisation Facility's numerous publications and reports on the Syrian economy.

[7] Pareto-improving liberalization refers to policy that does not eliminate benefits for some economic actors while granting economic benefits to others. It attempts to create 'winners' without creating 'losers'.

[8] Article 51 of Law 23 (2002) creating the CMC states that "the Syrian Central Bank is a public institution with financial and administrative autonomy in charge of implementing monetary policy to be determined by the Monetary and Credit Council, operating under the auspices of the State within the general orientations of the economy policy adopted by the Council of Ministers."

[9] See document entitled 'The Framework for Financial Sector Reform in Syria' (2006) published by the State Planning Commission.

---

[10] Based on a survey of Syrian businesses, the World Bank (2005: 31) has determined that 70% of firm interactions with tax inspectors involve informal payments.

2
Growth in Transition and Syria's Economic Performance

Ferdinand Arslanian

Introduction

This paper attempts to analyze Syria's economic performance within the framework of a transition economy where economic performance is determined through the interaction of the country's initial conditions at the outset of transition with its liberalization measures and macroeconomic stabilization policies rather than by traditional supply side factor inputs such as capital and labor. It must be acknowledged that it is somewhat problematic to refer to Syria as a "planned economy", and, consequently, its subsequent gradual economic liberalization as a "transition economy". Perthes (1992), for example, was cautious in labeling Syria a "planned economy" "as the plans lacked virtually any compulsory force' (Perthes 1992: 45). Hinnebusch (1995) viewed Syria's economic policy as more neo-mercantilist than state capitalist, aimed at state formation through external rents rather than seeking to maximize capital accumulation. This aspect questions the whole rationality of applying a transition model developed by reference to the transition experience of the central planning economies of the socialist bloc to Syria's creeping economic liberalization.

On the other hand, it could be argued that central planning economies are highly heterogonous among themselves; with the main difference being between East Asian and European countries, and within European Countries between the former Soviet Union and Eastern European Countries. Therefore, by comparing and contrasting Syria's economic performance with that of other transition countries, and by classifying Syria's economy among the different categories of transition countries with regards to its initial conditions, reform strategy and performance, the relevance of the transition model as an analytical tool for the Syrian economy, in addition to its special features, could be identified. Furthermore, the analysis will identify where Syria currently stands in its process of transition to a market economy and, consequently, what lies ahead for the country. Therefore, by considering Syria's foreign exchange crisis in 1986 and its subsequent reform policies as a starting point for Syria's transition into a market economy, this paper finds that the transition model is quite relevant for explaining Syria's economic performance. Syria can be categorized as an underdeveloped resource abundant transition country, and therefore initially enjoyed a fast recovery, and consequently delayed reforms and was locked in a staple trap[1]. And now with the gradual decline of its oil reserves, the Syrian economy is being exposed to its accumulated weaknesses, suffering from low adminsitrative capacity to implement reforms, a weak industrial base and a constrained business environment.

This paper is organized as follows. Section 2 provides an overview of the Syrian economy during its central planning years up to the foreign exchange crisis in 1986. In section 3 an analysis of Syria's initial conditions in comparison with other transition countries will be carried out after explaining the impact of initial conditions on liberalization and economic performance according to de Melo et al (1997). The years from 1986 onwards are sub-divided into three periods based on their distinct characteristics in terms of structural reforms and performance. Therefore, section 4 examines the austerity years of (1986-1990), while section 5 illustrates the decade of economic pluralism in the nineties. Finally, section 6 attempts to outline the developments of the period from 2000 onwards.

Central Planning in Syria

The first glimpse of central planning in Syria took place during Syria's union with Egypt in 1958, with land redistribution, bank nationalization and an increase in the role of the state taking place. Later on in the 1960s and with the rise of the Ba'th party to power, more radical reforms were undertaken with a series of nationalizations of private firms and a bigger role for the state in production, redistribution and consumption. The period 1966-1970 witnessed an attempt to launch a huge program of public investment and to expand the manufacturing sector. However, this attempt was curtailed by the lack of domestic financial resources due to the flight of private capital and the erratic performance of public industrial enterprises. Public investments concentrated on two mega projects (the Euphrates dam and initiating petroleum production) that absorbed the majority of public resources, leading to increases in inflation rates and foreign debt and causing bottlenecks in the supply of many goods.

However, this ambitious program of public investment began to materialize in the 70s with the flow of external funds from various sources: Arab aid, oil exports, remittances and transit revenue, in addition to the availability of cheap credit in the international market. Investments were projected in industry and infrastructure such as dams and power stations. Development in the form of electricity, roads and schools was noticeable in all parts of the country. Public industry was based on consumer-oriented import substitution industrialization (ISI) which was highly dependent on advanced imported technology, raw material and spare parts (Perthes 1992, pp. 40). Furthermore, the implementation of this massive investment program resulted in the enlargement in the size of the government and its administrative institutions. On the other hand, the early seventies witnessed the revival of the private sector. However, this new private sector was highly marginalized, acting as a sub-contractor to the large state sector and specializing in peripheral activities such as construction, real estate speculation and exports-imports operations. Overall, during the seventies - as argued by Hinnebusch (1995) - the state controlled the heights of the economy while the private sector was confined to the periphery.

However, many problems became apparent with import substitution industrialization, with many plants not going into operation upon completion due to the lack of local expertise (Perthes 1992, pp. 40). Moreover, ISI led to an increase in imports of intermediate goods, increasing the pressure on the countries' balance of payments. Furthermore, the over-centralization (the lack of operational authority for plant managers) and politicization (achieving maximum employment, political appointments) of public plants deprived them of dynamism, resulting in weak financial performance and rendering them unable to generate sufficient surpluses for financing major investments (Hinnebusch 1995, pp. 309). Nevertheless, the lack of profitability of the public sector neither deterred its expansion nor induced its reconstruction. The public sector was sustained with the facilitation of abundant external rents, and the state bureaucracy and army kept on expanding, creating a state too large for its economic base. And with the decline in Arab aid, oil prices and remittances in the eighties, the crisis in the Syrian economy began to materialize. The increase in the import of capital goods and spare parts induced by ISI, in addition to the increase in the import of agricultural food imports all contributed to the widening of the balance of payments deficit and the increase in foreign debt leading to a foreign exchange crisis in 1986 which would bring on many reform measures and could be considered as the starting year of transition in our analysis.

Figure 2.1 Syria's Average Annual GDP Growth Rates (%)

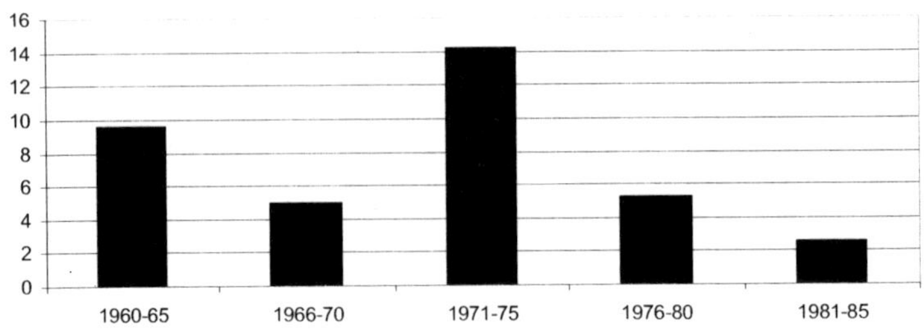

Source: Central Bureau of Statistics, Various Editions

The crisis was most obvious in the declining growth rates of Syrian GDP throughout the second half of the 70s and the first half of the 80s (figure 2.1). Thus, while the average annual growth rates in the first half of the 70s reached 14%, they declined to around 5% in the second half and then again to 2.6% in the first half of the 80s.

The main difference in Syria's central planning experience in comparison with the standard central planning economy (CPE) lies in the following: CPEs were successful in their early years in achieving high growth rates due to their successful accumulation of factor inputs, capital and labor. They were successful at mobilizing rural labor surpluses from agriculture into industry, and at achieving high domestic savings rates and allocating them into productive investment. And with the exhaustion of rural labor surplus and the limitations on increasing the investment ratio, CPE growth declined due to the failure of increasing total factor productivity. On the other hand, the public sector in Syria, from the very beginning, had failed to become "an engine of capital accumulation" (Hinnebusch 1995, pp. 309) and its high investment and expenditure levels relied on external sources rather than on domestic savings. Therefore, with the decline of these sources, growth rates plummeted even before the exhaustion of rural labor surplus. In other words, in Syria "the economic logic of accumulation was subordinated to the logic of state formation" (Hinnebusch 1995, pp. 311) leading to the overdevelopment of the state without having a profound industrial base to maintain it. Therefore, while CPEs have been successful in changing the structure of their economies from a rural based economy to an industrial one, Syria's economic structure remained highly stagnant with a slight increase in industry, due to oil production, and in services, due to the increase in government services.

Table 2.1 Structure of GDP in Market Prices by Sector (at constant prices of 1985)

	1963	1970	1975	1980	1985
Agriculture	35	24	22	25	21
Industry	15	22	22	20	22
Services	50	54	56	55	57

Source: Central Bureau of Statistics (1990)

Initial Conditions

De Melo et al (1997) identify 11 variables that characterize the initial conditions of transition economies in their shift towards market oriented development. These indicators are clustered into two groups. The first group (PRIN1) represents the degree of macroeconomic distortions which is based on the degree of trade dependency, repressed inflation and black market premium. These distortions are assumed to be translated into shocks to the economy as liberalization takes place and therefore measure the intensity of transitory shocks.[2] Also included is the extent of familiarity of market processes and experience as a coherent nation-state, counterbalancing factors that measure the likely capacity of a state to deal with distortions. The second group (PRIN2) represents the overall level of development, with countries ranking high on this index tending to have a higher per capita income and a higher share of urban population and suffering from over-industrialization, diminishing returns to investment and low pre-reform growth rates. Plotting transition countries against these two groups, four broad clusters emerge, indicated in table 3.1. It should be noted that initial conditions, along with other variables, have their influence on performance through two channels; 1) directly and 2) indirectly through its impact on liberalization. The links between initial conditions, policy

Table 3.1 Classifying Transition Countries According to their Initial Conditions

Clusters	Countries	Level of Development	Macroeconomic Distortions
1	Baltic States- Russia – Caucasus	High	High
2	East European Countries	High	Low
3	Central Asian States	Low	High
4	China-Vietnam-Albania	Low	Low

reform choices given by the liberalization indices,[3] and performance outcomes measured in terms of growth and inflation, have been identified through the following system of equations; where "i" represents country and "t" represents year:[4]

LIBit = a + bo LIB it-1 + b1 PRIN1i + b2 PRIN2i + b3 FREEDOMit + b4 RTit + e (1)

PERFORMANCEit = z + y0 PRIN1i + y1 PRIN2i + y2 LIBit +y3 LIB it-1 + y4 RT it + e (2)

Beginning with the performance equation, the model predicts, based on previous empirical results,"that good performance (high growth, low inflation) depends negatively on the size of the contemporaneous liberalization step (LIB) but positively on the accumulated stock of reforms (LIB-1)", and therefore $y2 < 0$, $y3 > 0$. Regarding initial conditions, the model predicts that both macroeconomic distortions (PRIN1) and the level of development (PRIN2) –capturing structural distortions such as overindustrialization - have negative effects on performance ($y0 < 0$, $y1 < 0$). The model predicts a negative relation between the level of macroeconomic distortions (PRIN1) and the degree of liberalization, ($b1 < 0$), consistant with the behavior of output smoothing since both PRIN1 and contemporaneous liberalization have a negative impact on performance. On the other hand, it is expected that the PRIN2 is positively correlated with the degree of liberalization, ($b2 > 0$), since countries with higher levels of development have greater administrative capacity to implement reform and a greater capacity to absorb negative shocks. The model also addresses regional tensions (RT) and political freedom (FREEDOM) where it assumes that higher regional tension and the absence of political freedom will both have a negative impact on performance and liberalization ($b3 < 0$, $y3 < 0$, $b4 > 0$, $y4>0$). The model explains why East European Countries (the second cluster) exhibiting a high degree of over-industrialization and modest economic distortions will liberalize and recover faster than countries in the first cluster (Russia and the Baltics) or than Central Asian countries in the third cluster. Moreover, it explains why the two East Asian countries in cluster 4, with low level of development and limited economic distortions, can grow fast despite pursuing a gradual reform strategy.

Below the analysis will address Syria's initial conditions in comparison with other transition countries and try to identify where Syria is positioned among these clusters and accordingly attempt to predict the impact of its initial conditions on its transition strategy as illustrated by de Melo et al (1997).

Overall level of development

Income levels[5] *(PPP in base years)*[6]

Examining figure 3.1, we note that transition countries varied widely in their per capita income at the outset of transition, from Slovenia (9200$)

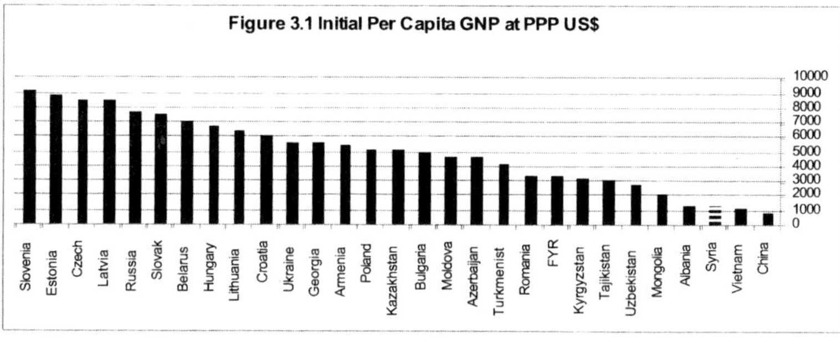

Source: De Melo et al (1997), World Development Indicators

to China (800$). In comparison with other transition economies, Syria's initial per capita income, at (1382 US$), is considered very low, ranking third among the lower end of transition countries, only exceeding the levels of East Asian countries (China 800 US$ – Vietnam 1100 US$), and slightly lower than Albania's per capita income (1400 US$).

Urbanization

The percentage of urban population also varies widely among different transition countries, with Russia having the highest percentage of urban population (74% of the total population) and Asian countries having the lowest percentage with less than 20% of their population being urban (figure 3.2). In the case of Syria, its urban population constituted 49% of

Figure 3.2 Urbanization (% of Population)
Initial year of reform

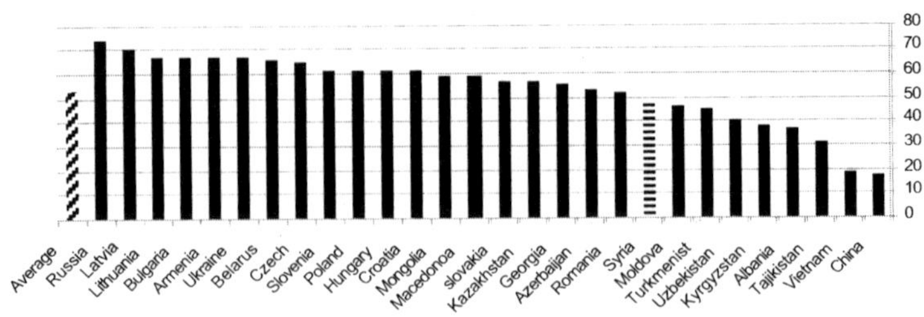

Source De Melo et al (1997), Central Bureau of Statistics (1987)

total population, the ninth least urbanized country in our set of transition economies, and slightly lower than the transition economies' average (54%).

Since urbanization also acts as a proxy for the level of development, its cross-country distribution is supposed to closely mirror that of income levels as argued by De Melo et al (1997) with lower income countries being on average more rural. Although this argument applies for Syria, its urbanization level is somehow high in comparison with its income level. Thus, while Syria's income level is comparable with that of Albania and Vietnam and lower than all Central Asian countries' income levels, its share of urban population surpasses the share of Asian countries, Albania and most of the Central Asian countries (only Kazakhstan has a higher urban percentage of the population at 57%)

Industrialization

Industrialization is another indicator that proxies for the level of development. A common feature of socialist countries was overindustrializtion, as the share of industry in GDP was high because services were typically repressed. Nevertheless, Syria's GDP structure, at the eve of reform, was quite contrary to the typical socialist country, as it had the lowest share of industry in GDP and one of the highest shares of services among transition countries (figures 3.3 and 3.4).

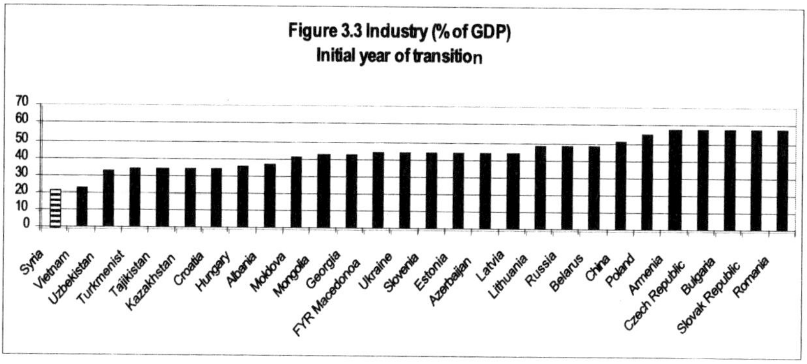

Source: de Melo et al (1997), Central Bureau of Statistics (1987)

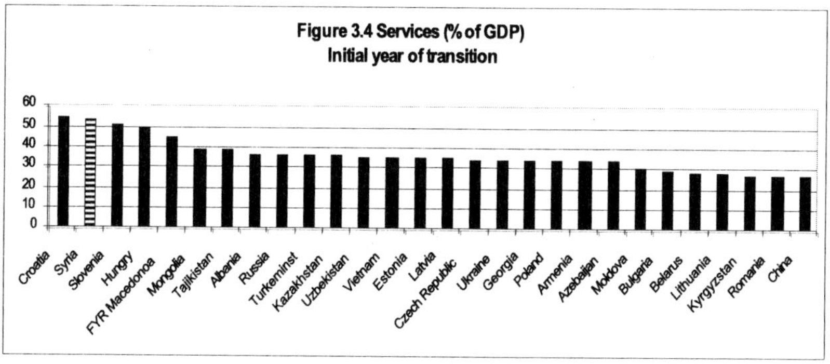

Source: de Melo et al (1997), Central Bureau of Statistics (1987)

Richness of natural resources

Originally natural resource abundance was viewed as a facilitator of transition by preventing the negative terms of trade shock associated with energy importers after the breaking up of the CMEA system (de Melo et al 1997, pp. 11). Later on, more emphasis was directed towards the effects of resource abundance on delaying reforms, feeding corruption and retarding economic diversification (Auty 1999). Turning to Syria, it was moderately rich in natural resources, possessing 0.53 hectares per capita cropland in 1986, and reasonable gas and oil reserves, in addition to minerals like phosphates.

Prior economic growth rates

Based on the observance that growth in CPEs tends to be higher at their earlier stages, mature countries were likely to experience stagnation, whereas poorer countries were still expected to benefit from higher growth (de Melo et al 1997, pp. 12). However, the logic above is notrelevant for Syria- a poor country- since its prior economic growth rates (2.7% on a five year average) lag behind its comparators with low income levels (China 9%, Mongolia 5.4%, Vietnam 5%, Uzbekistan 3.9%, and Albania 3.6%). Furthermore, by taking a four years average (1982-1985) growth rate, instead of a five years average (1981-1985), Syria will have an even lower prior economic growth rate at only 1%. Therefore, it seems as if Syria's growth capacity under central planning has reached its limitations in spite of its low level of development.

Figure 3.5 Prior Economic Growth Rates
Five years average growth rates prior to transition

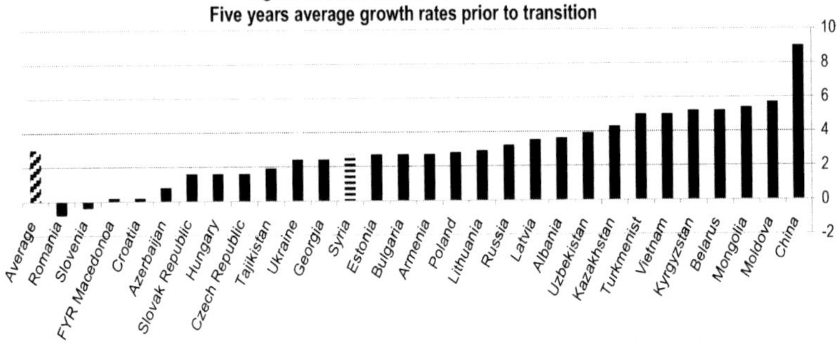

Source: de Melo et al (1997), Central Bureau of Statistics (1987)

Conclusion

On the eve of transition, Syria was highly underdeveloped with a very low level of per capita income and industrialization, only comparable with East Asian transition countries. On the other hand, there were many features that were quite contrary to a country with a low level of development. Syria's higher than expected share of urban population, its economy dominated by services and suffering from low growth rates, all come in contrast with a typical poor socialist country. If anything, Syria was showing signs of early maturity relative to the length of its central planning years.

Level of Macro-economic Distortion

As Syria's transition was sparked by a foreign exchange crisis, the economy was suffering from quite severe macroeconomic imbalances,[7] with both fiscal deficit and foreign debt exceeding 20% of GDP. Nevertheless, Syria's black market exchange rate premium of 282 (figure 3.2), although considered high by international standards, was still below the average rate of transition countries (469). Moreover, Syria (figure 3.7) was highly trade dependant (28% of GDP comparing with an average of 19.7% for transition countries) and integrated with the CMEA system (46% of overall exports and 20% of overall imports) at the outset of reform, making it highly vulnerable to a large external shock associated with the breakdown of CMEA trade (figures 3.8 and 3.9)

Figure 3.6 Black Market Exchange Rate Premium

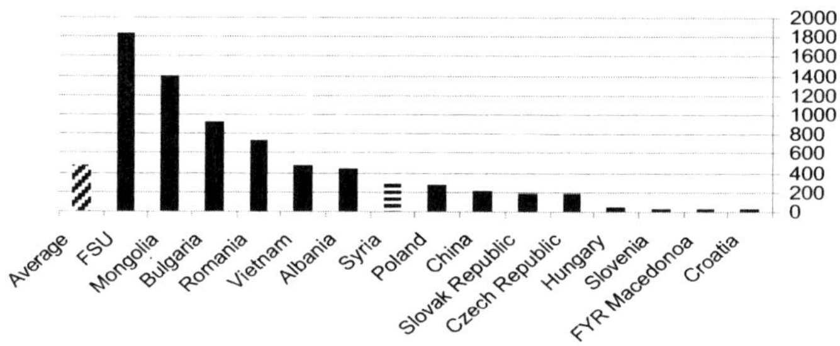

Source: De Melo e al (1997), Central Bureau of Statistics (1987)

Figure 3.7 Trade Dependence (%of GDP)
Initial year of transition

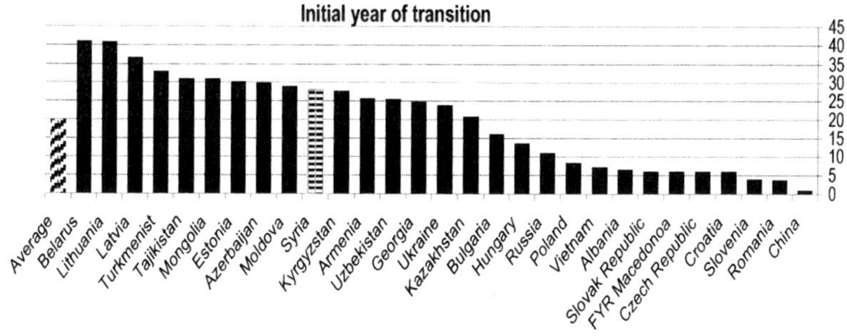

Source: De Melo et al (1997), Jooni (2001)

Figure 3.8 Distribution of Syrian Exports by International Blocs 1986

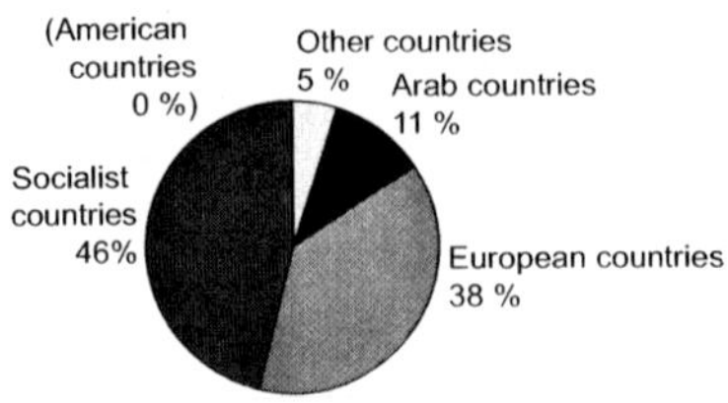

Figure 3.9 Distribution of Syrian Imports by International Blocs 1986

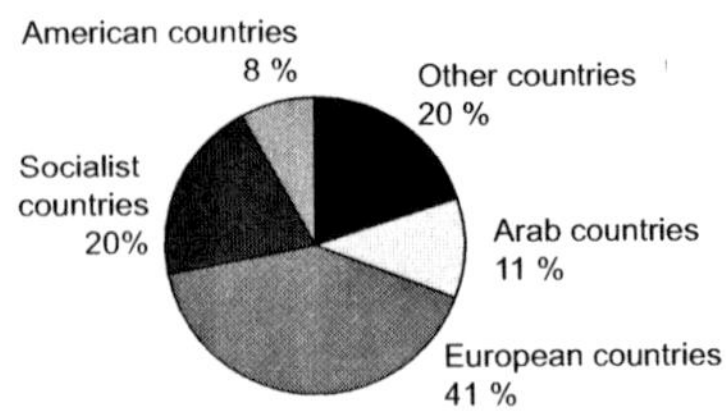

Source: Central Bureau of Statistics (1987)

Syria's geographic *location* is problematic. Whereas Syria is in a good location to serve the large markets of Europe and the oil-rich Arab countries, regional instability constrains its ability to exploit its geographical advantage. Furthermore, at the time of its transition, oil-rich Arab countries were suffering from declining oil prices while European countries where nowhere near achieving the high growth rates that East Asian countries were enjoying and which benefited China and Vietnam.

Institutional characteristics (Stateness, Market Memory):

With regards to the initial institutional characteristics of transition economies, two variables capture these effects: stateness and market memory. Syria was an independent state prior to transition and, therefore, did not need to establish new national and economic institutions during the economic challenges of transition, by contrast with former Yugoslav or former Soviet republics.

Assuming that central planning began in Syria in 1963, Syria had experienced 23 years under central planning (figure 3.10), a very short period in comparison with other transition countries with only Vietnam spending a shorter period (21 years). As such, Syria enjoys a stronger memory of market oriented systems. Furthermore, as in Vietnam, a substantial - although marginalised - private sector continued to exist in industrial production and in some services sectors. And despite public control over production and distribution of agricultural products, agricultural production was dominated by medium and small-sized farmers since agrarian reform had never led to collectivisation, and had resulted instead in the disappearance of traditional large-scale landowners and the fragmentation of their property.

Figure 3.10 Years under Central Planning

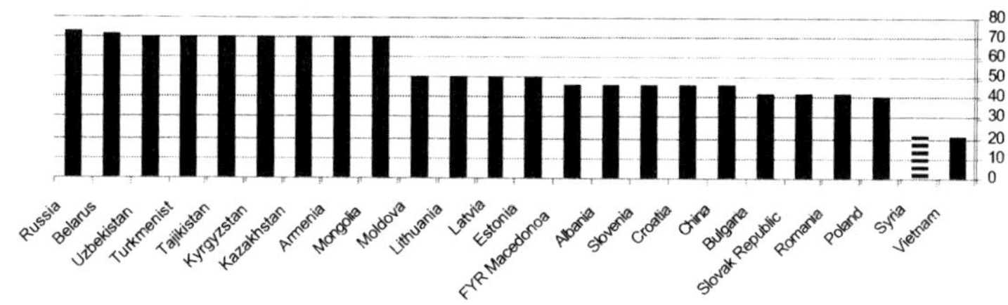

Source: de Melo et al (1997)

Therefore, based on the De Melo et al (1997) criteria, Syria enjoyed favorable initial institutional characteristics being an independent state prior to reform, spending a short period under central planning and maintaining a significant private sector. However, if measures of the quality of government are to be included such as indexes for corruption and democratization, or tax collection ability, Syria's initial institutional characteristics would seem less favorable.

Overall, it is quite clear that Syria has a low level of development making it belong to either cluster 3 or cluster 4. It is unclear, however, whether Syria is positioned within cluster 3 or 4 as its macro distortion is moderately high while its institutional characteristics are favorable. However, it is safe to assume that Syria was less distorted than Central Asian countries and more distorted than East Asian countries, placing it somewhere close to the borders of the two clusters Table 3.2).

Table 3.2 Syria's Set of Initial Conditions in Comparison with Clusters 3 & 4 as Identified by de Melo et al (1997)

	Syria	Cluster 4	Cluster 3
Overall level of development			
Income levels (PPP in base years)	Low	Low	Low
Urbanization	Low	Low	Low
Industrialization	Low	Low	Low
Richness of natural resources	Rich	Rich	Rich
Prior economic growth rates	Low	High	High
Level of macroeconomic distortions			
Repressed inflation/fiscal deficit	High	Low	High
Trade shares in GDP	High	Low	High
Black market exchange rate premium	Medium	Low	High
Location proximity to thriving markets	Medium	Good	Poor
Institutional Characteristics			
State	Independent	Independent	New nation
Market memory	High	High	Low

Applying the model mentioned above to Syria shows (table 3.3) that, with exception of its high initial accumulated stock of reform, all other factors will negatively affect the pace of liberalization and therefore Syria is more likely to adopt a policy of gradual reform.

Table 3.3 Predicting the Impact of Different Factors on Syria's Pace of Liberalization and Economic Performance according to de Melo et al (1997)

Effect on the Pace of Liberalization		Effect on Performance	
High macro distortions	-	High macro distortions	-
Low level of development	-	Low level of development	+
High initial accumulated stock of reform	+	Low degree of contemporaneous liberalization + High accumulated stock of reform	+
Absence of political freedom	-		
High regional tensions	-	High regional tensions	-

On the other hand, it is hard to predict the final outcome of Syria's performance since it is not clear whether the negative factors (macro distortions and regional tension) will outweigh the positive factors (low level of development and the combination of high accumulated stock of reform with a low degree of contemporaneous liberalization). The following chapters will show how well the model and other stylized facts of growth in transition fit in with the case of Syria.

The Austerity Years 1986-1990

Liberalization measures

The reforms taken by the Syrian government had a rather tentative nature as there had been no clear commitment to switch to a market economy. These reforms aimed at coping with the fiscal and financial crisis rather than implementing a comprehensive transition strategy; despite that, the results 'tended to create a more liberal and capital oriented economy' (Perthes 1992, pp. 43).

Therefore, the nature of the crisis, as a fiscal and financial one, shaped the applied liberalization measures. On one hand, the fiscal crisis, as noted by Hinnebusch (1995), forced the regime to reduce its economic responsibilities and seek a private sector alternative, setting its eyes on mobilizing the enormous expatriate and hidden local capital. On the other hand, the foreign exchange crisis encouraged export promotion and opened international trade to the private sector. Several reforms were characteristic of this period.

Fiscal Austerity: The austere public policy that the government began to implement in 1981 intensified and the budget declined from around 50% of GDP in 1985 to nearly 30% in 1987. The curtailing of government expenditure was achieved through implementing a harsh wage policy, introducing cuts in public subsidies and bringing the expansion of public enterprises to a halt.

Liberalization of Agriculture: With the aim of reducing public expenditure and increasing agricultural production, the Syrian government started to gradually reform its agricultural policy, switching from central to indicative planning. Compulsory delivery of major crops to public sector organizations was relaxed in 1987, and prices - based on an estimate of production costs plus a profit margin - were introduced as a tool for delivering crops. Starting from 1988, subsidies for agricultural inputs such as jute bags, seeds and chemical fertilizers were gradually eliminated. Moreover, restrictions on private sector agricultural exports were relaxed and public-private joint ventures of agricultural companies were encouraged. And by 1990, compulsory deliveries for major agricultural products had been abolished while foreign trade had been liberated regarding the export of vegetables, fruits, chickens, eggs and natural juice. Furthermore, the private sector assumed a greater role in the production, distribution and export of agricultural products. However, the gradual reduction of subsidies for farm inputs was matched by a greater increase in the prices of farm products.

Opening investment and foreign trade to the private sector: The government first promoted private investment in tourism and agriculture (Law no. 10 /1986), using tax exemptions and trade facilitations. It also revoked a ban imposed on the private sector's participation in certain industries formerly reserved for the public sector (Decree of the Ministry of Industry in 1987). Moreover, the government gradually began to abandon its monopolies on foreign trade. The private sector was allowed to import a set of goods using export revenues, with a share of these revenues being delivered to the Commercial Bank of Syria at an official rate, while for another set of goods, the private sector was allowed to import on the basis of the so-called "credit facilities", which in practice meant that the public sector did not deliver the necessary currencies for imports which importers had to find by their own covert means (Economic Research Forum 2006, pp. 59). These measures encouraged fictive exports[8] and implicitly recognized the informal exchange rate market. Most importantly, the authorities made a barter deal (1988- 1990) with the Soviet-Union in order to repay its debts. Within this deal, the private sector was encouraged to export all kinds of goods. On the other hand, the foreign exchange system became even more complex with the introduction of multiple exchange rates in foreign trade and the development of several regimes of importing procedure depending on the goods involved (Economic Research Forum 2006, pp. 59).

Performance

GDP path:
The clearest differences in the performance of transition countries are between the countries of East Asia, China and Vietnam, and the countries of Central and Eastern Europe and the Former Soviet Union. All CEE and FSU countries experienced initial output decline and most have experienced hyperinflation. In contrast, China and Vietnam did not experience any initial output decline and benefited from continuous high growth rates. Moreover, East Asian countries have been successful in containing inflation. This initial output decline in non-Asian transition countries and the recovery afterwards is considered one of the most defined stylized facts of transition, and is usually termed as the U shape curve.

Figure 4.1 GDP Path in Transition Time
(pre-transition year = 100)

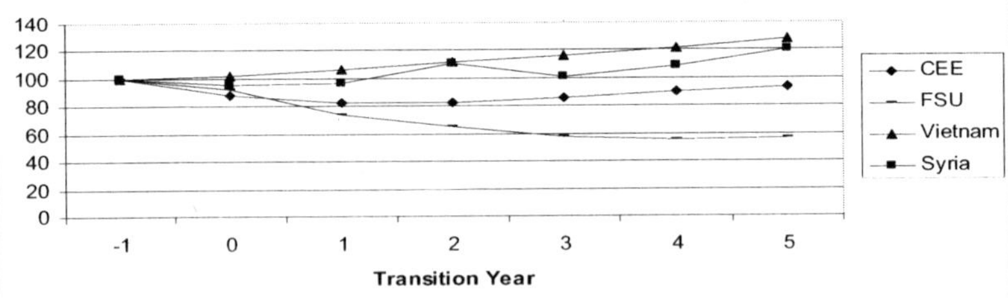

Source: Central Bureau of Statistics (1993), Arkadie and Mallon (2003), World Development Indicators (2003)

The question to be asked is whether Syria's initial output performance is closer to that of CEE and FSU countries or Asian countries. Has Syria experienced the U shape curve? Or has it experienced continuous high growth rates? The question is quite interesting since Syria had a low level of development comparable with that of Asian countries and also a similar high market memory. On the other hand, Syria had experienced more severe initial macro-imbalances compared with the two Asian Transition economies.

Based on Syria's output performance of the first five years after reform (1986-1990), as in figure 4.1, we notice that instead of both the conventional U shape curve of CEE and FSU countries and the continuous high growth rates of Asian countries, Syria experienced quite a non-conventional W shape curve with output declining only in the first year (1986), and recovering its 1985 level in the third year (1988), while collapsing again in the fourth year (1989) – although not lower than its 1985 level - and rising again in fifth year (1990). In comparison with other transition countries, Syria had the lowest cumulative output decline of 4.95% of pre-transition GDP (figure 4.2).

Figure 4.2 Cumulative Output Decline to Lowest Level

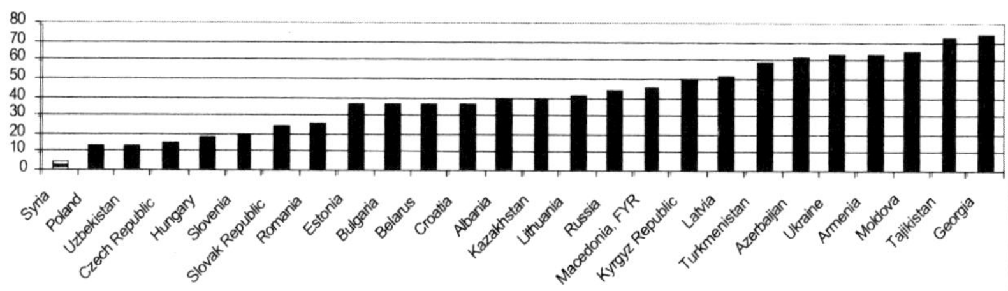

Source: Fisher and Sahay (2000)-Central Bureau of Statistics (1993)

Gross Fixed Capital Formation:

Syria's gross fixed capital formation as a percentage of GDP plummeted from 24% in 1985 to reach its lowest level at 14% of GDP in 1988 only to rise again to around in 16% of GDP in 1989 and 1990. Most importantly, the austerity years witnessed a clear change in the contribution of the public and private sectors to gross fixed capital formation in favor of the private sector. The contribution of the public sector saw a continuous decline from around 16% of GDP in 1985 to around 7% of GDP in 1990. The share of the private sector, in absolute terms, did not change significantly throughout the period (8% of GDP in 1985 to 9% in 1990) despite a sharp decrease to 5% of GDP in 1988. However, in relative terms, there was a significant increase in the share of the private sector in gross fixed capital formation, from 34% in 1985 to 55% in 1990, while the share of the public sector declined from 66% in 1985 to 45% in 1990 (Figure 4.3). Thus the relative increase in the share of the private sector in gross fixed capital formation can be attributed to the absolute decline in the public sector's gross fixed capital formation. This trend is compatible with the stylist facts of transition countries where investment falls more than GDP, and thus investment rates decline (Compos and Coricelli 2002, pp. 803).

Figure 4.3 Gross Fixed Capital Formation in Syria (1985-1990) (% of GDP)

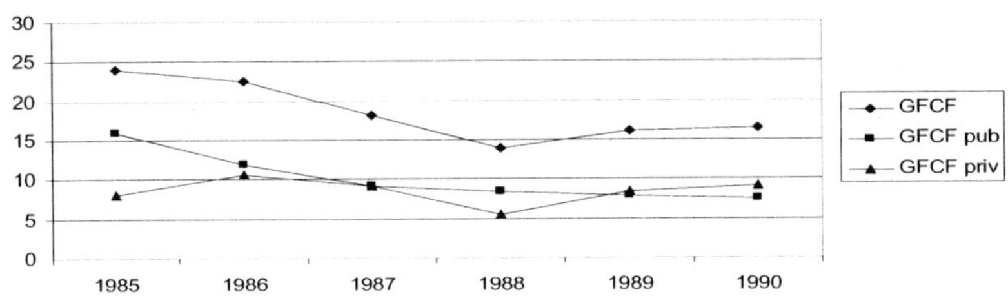

Source: Central Bureau of Statistics (1993)

Structural changes in the Syrian economy

Examining the sectoral changes in GDP throughout the period (1985-1990), we note that the share of agriculture, although volatile from a year to year basis, remained constant at around 20% of GDP. While the share of industry dropped from 22% in 1985 to 20% in 1986, and afterwards increased dramatically to reach 32% of GDP in 1990. On the other hand, the share of services declined dramatically from 57% of GDP in 1985 to 48% of GDP in 1990 (Table 4.1).

These changes come in contrast with the structural changes that usually occur in transition where the economy witnesses a process of de-industrialization and a boom in the suppressed services sector (Compos and Coricelli 2002, pp. 812). These changes even contrast with the experience of Vietnam which also witnessed a decrease in its share of industry and an increase in its share of services at a similar stage of transition (Van Arkadie and Dinh 2004, pp. 25).

Table 4.1 Structure of Syrian GDP 1985-1990

(In constant prices of 1985)

	Agriculture	**Industry**	**Services**
1985	21	22	57
1986	23	20	56
1987	20	21	59
1988	23	24	53
1989	18	30	52
1990	20	32	48

Source: Central Bureau of Statistics (1993)

By disaggregating the services sector (table 4.2), it can be noted that only the transportation and communications sub-sector and the negligible private non-profit services sector had positive effects on the share of services in GDP, while the four other sub-sectors (trade, finance and insurance, social services and government services) all had negative effects on its share. The biggest two sub-sectors in 1985, trade (22.2%) and government services (17.3%), had the highest share of decline of 4.32%, 3.83% of GDP respectively, by the end of 1990, with their contribution to the decline in the services sector being the largest at 47% and 41.6% respectively. Changes in the share of trade, for the period 1985-1990, were volatile and did not follow a clear trend, and its share only decreased significantly below its 1985 level in 1990 (these changes will be left unexplained here). The decline in the share of government services, which reached its lowest level in 1988 to 12% of GDP and increased slightly afterwards can be attributed to cuts in public expenditure. And by adding the decline in social services, a sector highly financed by the public sector, social and government services contributed to more than half of the decline in the share of the services in GDP. Therefore, the decline in the share of services in GDP can, to a large extent, be attributed to fiscal austerity and the contraction of the government's social responsibilities that took place during the period (1986-1990).

Table 4.2 The Composition of the Services Sector (% of GDP)

Year	Trade	Transportation communication	Finance insurance	Social services	Government services	Private non profit services
1985	22.2	9.8	5.0	2.6	17.3	0.07
1986	19.8	10.5	5.8	2.5	17.3	0.08
1987	27.2	11.0	4.9	1.9	14.1	0.08
1988	25.4	10.0	4.4	1.5	12.1	0.08
1989	20.6	11.1	4.3	1.4	14.5	0.10
1990	17.9	10.5	4.4	1.5	13.5	0.09
Overall Change	***-4.3***	***0.7***	***-0.6***	***-1.2***	***-3.8***	***0.02***
Contribution to the decline in the services sector	***47.0***	***-7.6***	***6.3***	***12.7***	***41.6***	***-0.2***

Source: Central Bureau of Statistics (1993)

Thus, while other transition countries witnessed a process of de-industrialization during its early years reflecting the degree of over-industrialization during central planning, Syria witnessed a process that could be referred to as 'de-servicification' also reflecting the over-ambitious state formation, in comparison with its level of development, which took place during the 70s. On the other hand, disaggregating industry is more problematic as mining and manufacturing are categorized in one sub sector and construction in another. Therefore, changes in manufacturing cannot be analyzed separately from changes in mining at the GDP level. However, data on mining and manufacturing are available separately at the NDP level at factor cost in current prices. At the GDP level, mining and manufacturing increased by 14.5 GDP percentage points during the period (1985-1990), while the share of building and construction decreased dramatically from 6.8% to 2.5% of GDP for the same period, due to the downsizing of the public construction companies (Perthes 1992: 44). At the NDP level, mining

	Table 4.3 The Composition of Industry				
	(% of GDP at market prices in constant prices of 1985)		(% of NDP at factor cost in current prices)		
Year	Mining & manufacturing	Building	Mining	Manufacturing	Mining & manufacturing
1985	15.0	6.8	6.9	6.3	13.1
1986	13.7	6.8	2.9	11.2	14.1
1987	17.3	3.7	7.5	5.9	13.5
1988	20.6	2.9	8.4	6.7	15.0
1989	27.5	2.7	12.8	8.9	21.7
1990	29.5	2.5	15.7	8.0	23.7
Overall Change	***14.5***	***-4.3***	***8.8***	***1.7***	***10.6***

Source: Central Bureau of Statistics, Various Editions

increased by 8.8 NDP percentage points while manufacturing increased by 1.7 NDP percentage points for the overall period. The highest share of increase in mining happened in the last two years (1989-1990), due to the hike in oil prices. And this sharp increase coincided with an increase in the share of manufacturing due to the implementation of the barter deal with the Soviet Union which encouraged manufacturing exports, explaining the dramatic increase in the share of industry towards the end of the period.

Trade

By examining figure 4.4, we note that imports declined from 22.6% of GDP to 17.2%, during the period (1985-1990), with the highest share of decline taking place in 1986 reflecting the foreign exchange crisis.

Figure 4.4 Syria's Foreign Trade (1985-1990) (% of GDP)

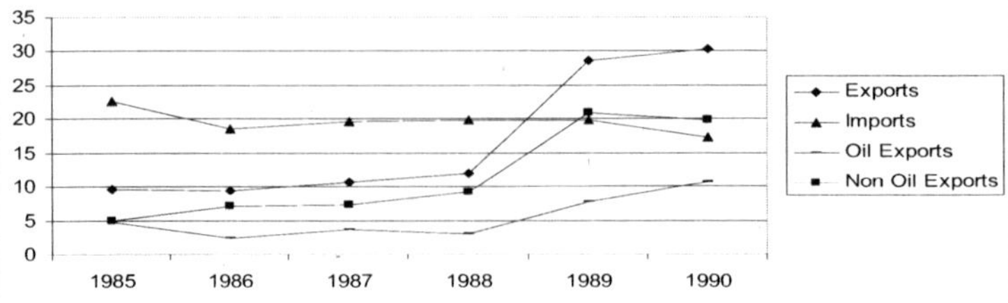

Source: Jooni (2001)

Exports increased from less than 10% of GDP in 1985 to around 30%. The hike in exports in 1989, obvious in the graph, reflects both an increase of around 12 GDP percentage points in non oil exports and 5 GDP percentage points in oil exports. The increase in oil exports is explained mainly by the rise in oil prices, while the increase in non oil exports could be explained by the export promotion strategy adopted by the government in order to acquire foreign currency, the barter deal with the Soviet Union for debt clearing, and partly by the development of 'fictive' exports with the aim of gaining legal access to foreign exchange,

Figure 4.5 Distribution of Syria's Exports by Economic Activity Classification (% of total exports)

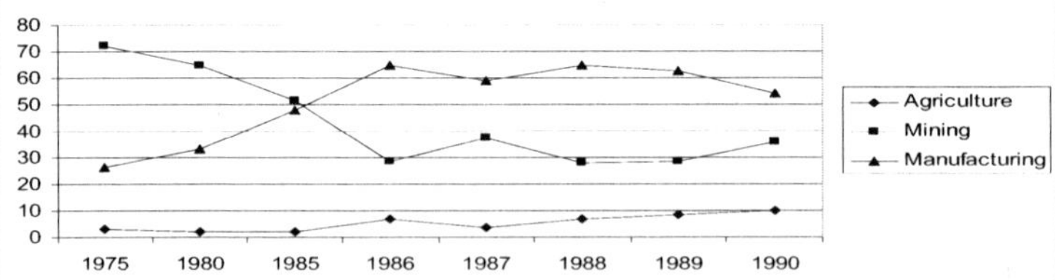

Source: Jooni (2001) - Central Bureau of Statistics, Various Editions

although it is difficult to disentangle these effects. It was manufacturing rather than mining that represented the highest share of exports (ranging between 55-65% of exports) although this might be misleading due to the development of fictive exports, as mentioned before. The increased opening of foreign trade to the private sector, and the encouragement of the private sector to participate in the Soviet barter deal led to significant increases in the contribution of the private sector to foreign trade. Thus, while the share of the private sector in overall exports was merely 8% and 16% in overall imports in 1985, its share, in 1990, increased to 45% and 46% respectively. Furthermore, by 1990, the private sector had the dominat role in exports agricultural (77%) and manufacturing (68%) exports (Although, as mentioned before, these figures are likely to overestimate private exports due to 'fictive' export and underestimate private imports as smuggling is not taken into account) (See table 4.4).

Table 4.4 The Share of the Private and Public Sectors in Foreign Trade

	Agricultural exports		Manufacturing exports		Total exports	
Year	Public	Private	Public	Private	public	Private
1985	73	27	86	14	92	8
1990	23	77	32	68	55	45
	Agricultural imports		Manufacturing imports		Total imports	
Year	Public	Private	Public	Private	public	Private
1985	94	6	77	23	84	16
1990	55	45	53	47	54	46

Source: Central Bureau of Statistics, Various Editions

Macroeconomic Stabilization

Overall, Syria was successful in achieving macroeconomic stabilization. The austerity measures and cuts in public spending assisted in reducing the budget deficit from 21% in 1984 to 3% in 1988. The combination of austerity level imports and increasing oil and non-oil exports led to a positive balance of payments surplus in 1989, or at least an ostensible balance of payments surplus. The first three years of reform (1986-1988) witnessed an increase in annual inflation above its average level (15%), due to the devaluation of the Syrian currency, the reduction of price subsidies and increasing shortages, which peaked at 53.2% in 1987. By 1989, inflation had been reduced significantly to 17%. The lowering of public spending and, consequently, the reduction in the fiscal deficit, the transferring of government borrowing from the Central Bank to the commercial banks and the increase in oil exports all contributed to reduction of inflation rates (figure 4.6). In comparison to other transition countries, the maximum annual inflation that Syria reached was relatively low, only higher than the rates of China, Hungry and the Czech Republic. Even if true inflation levels were higher than the levels reported – assuming actual inflation rates to be double that reported –Syria still did not experience the hyperinflation of other transition countries.

Figure 4.6 Syria's Annual Inflation Rates (%) (1984-1991)

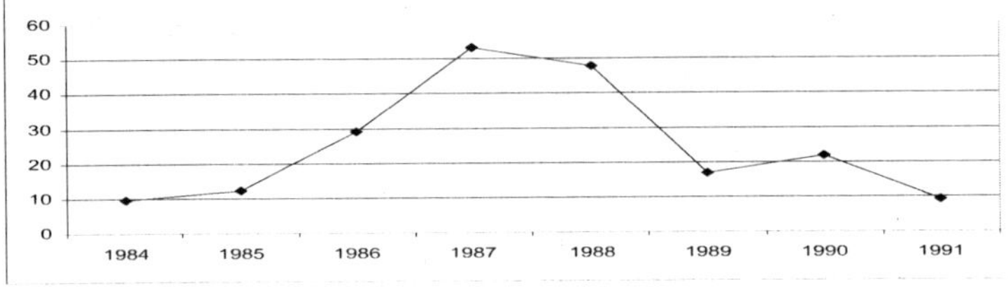

Source: Central Bureau of Statistics, Various Editions

Figure 4.7 Highest Annual Inflation Rates, Transition Countries

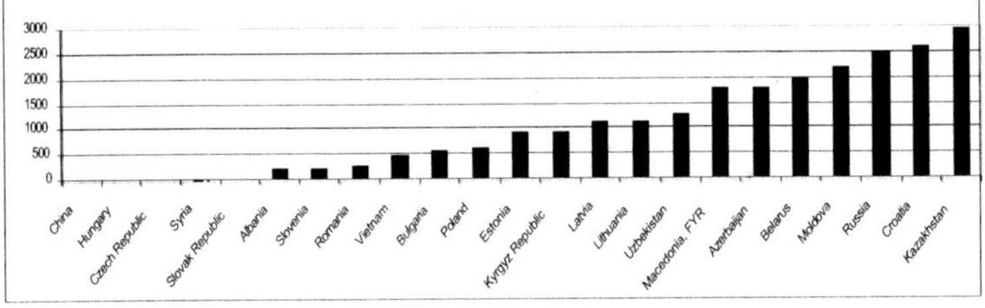

Source: Fisher and Sahay (2000) - Central Bureau of Statistics

Growth in Transition and Syria's Austerity Years

The initial low level of development and relatively high macroeconomic distortions in Syria led to the adoption of gradual and selective liberalization measures as predicted by the transition model, with liberalization confined to price liberalization, especially in agriculture, and increasing openness to the private sector in both investment and foreign trade; this resembles the dual track approach of Asian transition countries. Unlike Asian transition economies, however, Syria's favorable initial conditions (its low level of development and its strong market memory) were offset by the initial high levels of macroeconomic distortions (fiscal and balance of payments imbalances, high trade dependency and integration with the CMEA), increasing the predicted intensity of Syria's transitory shock. On the other hand, the existence of the Socialist bloc and the Soviet Union, at the time of reform, mitigated the adverse impact of a trade shock (especially with the export boom in manufacturing products to the Soviet Union 1988-1990 as a method of debt repayment). Furthermore, by taking the oil boom into account - or say, the increase in Syria's richness in natural resources - in addition to its gradual liberalization measures, it becomes clear why Syria's initial output decline was trivial in comparison with other transition countries. Therefore, the non-conventional W curve that characterized Syria's transitional output path could be explained, in addition to the factors mentioned above, by the volatility of the agricultural sector which was vulnerable to climate factors and undergoing a process of liberalization. Overall, recovery was achieved mainly through growth in oil exports rather than by the reallocation & restructuring mechanisms--that are stimulated through liberalization measures—necessary to recover from transformational recession. While Syria's investment ratio declined, in congruence with the stylized facts of transition countries, Syria's GDP structure did not change along the lines of other transition countries, indicating the special characteristics of Syria's central planning years.

The Nineties: Economic Pluralism

The end of the Gulf war initiated a new phase in the Syrian economy that lasted throughout the 1990s. The oil boom and the take off of the private sector could be regarded as the pillars of this new phase. The accumulated liberalization measures since the beginning of reform up to investment Law No.10 of 1991 stimulated the private sector; at the same time oil windfalls helped in sustaining the loss-making public sector and funded necessary infrastructure projects. This situation was denoted by the term "economic pluralism" which envisaged economic development through the encouragement of the public, mixed and private sectors.

Syrian manufacturing, after losing its soft export markets, due to the collapse of the Soviet block, became more oriented towards the domestic market. This tendency was facilitated by the new oil windfalls which provided necessary foreign exchange to import capital goods without facing a severe balance of payments deficit. Thus, the first half of the nineties witnessed the establishment of a manufacturing pattern that could be characterized as private-led, concentrating on consumer products and domestic-oriented. This pattern of industrialization was fortified by the oil windfalls and the trade restrictiveness of the Syrian trade regime. The initial success of this pattern diminished the incentive for further reforms, decreased the urge for competing in the international market and diminished the incentive for promoting manufacturing exports. Furthermore, the dynamics of this pattern of industrialization necessitated domestic market protection, thus, maintaining international trade restrictiveness. Thus, except for Investment Law No. 10 of 1991 liberalization was limited to the continuation of liberalization of the agricultural sector that was initiated in the late eighties.

Moving along to the macroeconomic stabilization policies that were pursued during the 90s, it should be noted that oil revenues assisted in financing the budget and stabilizing the exchange rate, and brought to a halt the decreasing trend in public expenditure that occurred during the austerity years. On the other hand, the fixed nominal interest rates immobilized monetary policy, leaving fiscal policy responsibility for price and exchange rate stability instead of concentrating on its role of influencing aggregate demand. Therefore, achieving budget equilibrium was of major concern. And taking into account the generous tax exemptions given to long term investment such as in Law No. 10 of 1991, achieving budget equilibrium necessitated maintenance of a still relatively contractionary expenditure policy which in turn had negative effects on aggregate demand. Thus, although Syria's inflation and fiscal position remained at manageable levels, this was achieved at the expense of stimulating aggregate demand (Economic Research Forum 2006, pp. 26).

The combination of deflationary fiscal policy and the absence of a second wave of reforms led to lower growth rates in the second half of the 90s. Thus, while the first half of the decade (1991-95) witnessed an average annual growth rate of 8.2%, the average annual growth rate of the second half of the decade (1996-2000) declined to 3.9%, and plummeting to -3.6% in 1999 (Central Bureau of Statistics, Various Editions). Moreover, the rise and fall of the private sector in Syria during the 90s is quite evident in the inverse 'U' shapes that characterized the trends of many variables. Private fixed capital formation (figure 5.1) increased from 10% of GDP in 1990 to 17% in 1994, only to decline again to 7.6% in 1999 (Central Bureau of Statistics, Various Editions). The same trend, the inverse 'U' curve, applies to private sector imports of capital goods during the 90s (figure 5.2). The share of manufacturing in GDP also increased during the first half of the decade to reach 13% in 1996, and declined in the second half to 4% of GDP in 2000 (Abu Ismail et al 2002, pp. 85).

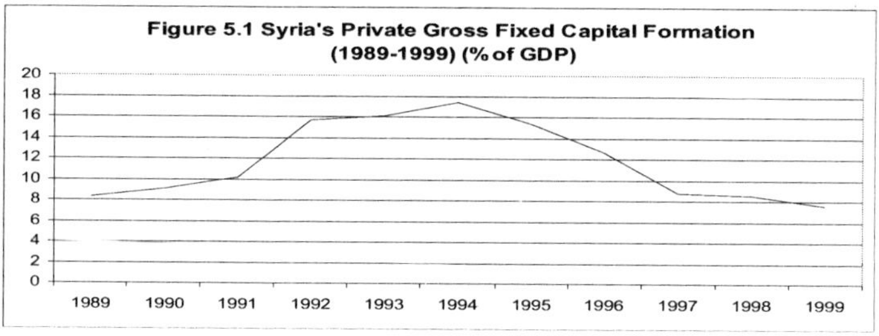

Source: Central Bureau of Statistics, Various Editions

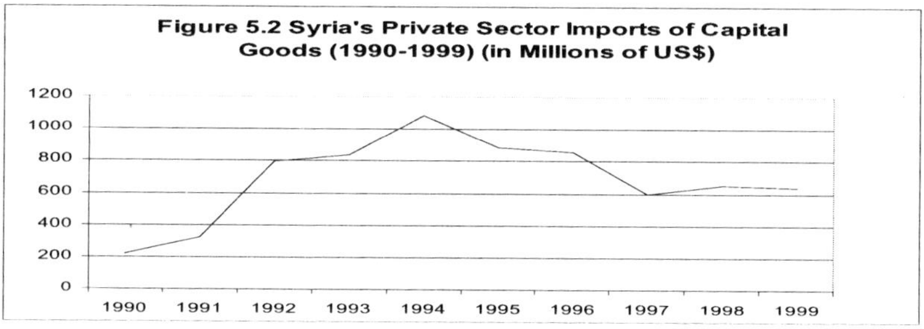

Source: Jooni (2001)

The absence of institutional and financial reforms made the cost of doing business in Syria exceptionally high and unpredictable. The private sector had limited access to finance and most firms relied on internal and family-based financing (World Bank 2005, pp. 39-40). The financial sector seemed weak and unable to allocate resources towards sectors in need. The highest percentage of loans was directed towards agriculture and distribution of agricultural products while manufacturing only captured a small fraction of overall loans (Table 5.1). Moreover, the over-regulated labor market, the high levels of informal payments, the unpredictable tax burden and inadequate infrastructure (electricity shortages-weak telecommunications infrastructure) all contributed to raising the cost and the unpredictability of doing business in Syria (World Bank, 2005). Furthermore, the weak protection of property rights, and the absence of marketing infrastructure hindered investing in research and innovation and targeting of export markets (World Bank, 2005).

Table 5.1 Allocation of Domestic Credit by Economic Sector: 1990-2000

	Agriculture	Wholesale and Distribution[9]	Industry and Mining	Construction	Services	Misc.	Total
1990	11%	73%	7%	6%	0%	2%	100%
1991	12%	72%	6%	7%	0%	2%	100%
1992	12%	72%	5%	7%	0%	3%	100%
1993	11%	70%	10%	7%	0%	2%	100%
1994	11%	73%	3%	9%	1%	3%	100%
1995	11%	71%	2%	9%	4%	3%	100%
1996	10%	71%	2%	10%	4%	3%	100%
1997	10%	71%	2%	10%	4%	3%	100%
1998	10%	70%	2%	10%	4%	3%	100%
1999	10%	72%	2%	10%	1%	6%	100%
2000	10%	72%	2%	9%	1%	6%	100%

Source: Central Bureau of Statistics, Various Editions

The absence of institutional and financial reforms deterred the natural expansion of the private sector which became locked in small enterprises (Hinnebusch 1995: 317). And although Investment Law No.10, with all its tax holidays, aimed at attracting local and foreign capital towards large scale manufacturing, the greatest bulk of investment concentrated on oil and services. Overall, the private sector was incapable of generating enough jobs to absorb excess labor, at a time when the public sector had reduced its responsibility as the major employment generator, leading to increasing unemployment and poverty. The long period of isolation from open markets had left Syria's industrial structure with enormous competitive gaps. By the end of the decade, "Syria suffered a technological downgrading of its production and exports structures," with the share of sophisticated products (high and medium technology) in Manufacturing Value Added falling from 10.5% in 1990 to 9.3% in 2000. The share of technological downgrading of manufactured exports was more even obvious, with the share of high and medium technology products in manufacturing exports plummeting from 28% in 1990 to 1% in 2000 (Albaladejo and Lull 2004, pp. 5-6).

Figure 5.3 Syria's Actual Public Expenditure (1990-2000) (% of GDP)

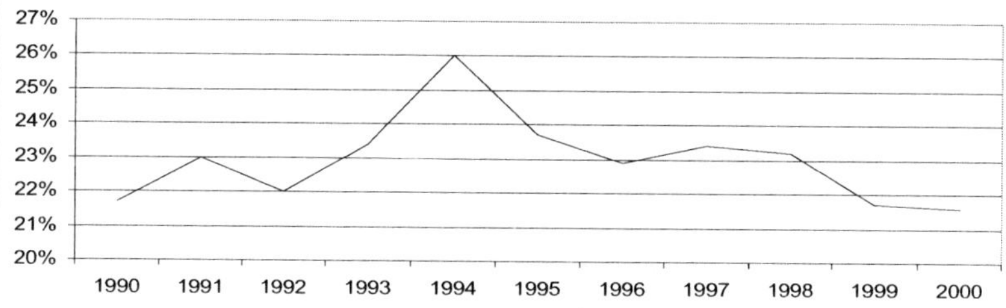

Source: Kanaan (2002)

On the other hand, the deflationary fiscal policy pursued by the government with the aim of achieving price and exchange rate stability led to a decline in actual public expenditure in the second half of the 90s, after peaking in 1994, at a time when fiscal stimulus was highly required (figure 5.3). Moreover, the fixed nominal interest rates at 8% played an important role in stimulating investment up to 1995 when inflation rates far exceeded interest rates, whereas after 1995, with the decline in inflation rates, fixed nominal interest rates hampered investments and contributed to the lower growth rates of the second half of the 90s (Kanaan, 2002). It must be noted that, within the framework above, exogenous factors which the Syrian economy is highly influenced by (rain-fed agriculture-oil-remittances) played either the role of cushioning (good harvest in 1998) or exposing (bad harvest - decline in oil revenues in 1999) the structural weaknesses in the Syrian economy during the second half of the decade.

Syria's boom in the early 90s can be attributed to the stabilization and liberalization measures taken in the late 1980s, thus confirming some of the most common consensuses in transition literature. One is that stabilization acts as a pre-condition for growth (Havrylyshyn 2001, pp. 68) and that it is through accumulated liberalization, given a time lag, that liberalization has a positive effect on growth (de Melo et al, 1997). Syria's boom in the early 90s also confirms the view that stimulating growth in the early stage of transition can be easily achieved by liberalization and stabilization. However, in the long run, institutional reform plays the decisive role in sustaining growth in transition. (Haverylyshyn and van Rooden 2000).

Moreover, Syria's experience confirms that the role of favorable initial conditions diminishes over time and growth cannot be sustained unless further liberalization measures are taken (de Melo et al 1997, pp. 35-37). On the other hand, Syria's success at achieving macro economic stabilization during the nineties was achieved at the expense of growth due to the peculiarity of Syria's fiscal and monetary policies, or say, the pre-maturity of Syria's fiscal and monetary policies. The experience of stabilization hampering growth in Syria comes in deep contrast with the positive role for it predicted in transition studies.

The anticipated trade shock associated with collapse of the Soviet bloc and the breakdown of the CMEA system was not materialized due to the increased oil exports to European countries. Thus, while exports to the former socialist countries plummeted to less than 10% of overall exports in 1992, exports to European countries soared to more than 60% (figure 5.4).

By comparing Syria's pattern of transition with other comparable low income transition countries such as Asian transition countries (Vietnam and China), it is noted that although both Syria and Asian countries adopted a gradual dual track approach to transition, there were many differences between the two experiences: whereas Syria isolated itself from the international market and concentrated on the domestic market, Vietnam and China, benefiting from their regional locations, sought to integrate their economies with the global market and follow an export led strategy. Although both Syria and Asian countries initiated economic reform without political change, political power in Asian countries was decentralized to local levels. Nothing similar to that has taken place in Syria. Vietnam and China have also been more successful in reforming their SOEs through imposing hard budget constraints, increasing enterprise autonomy and introducing profit based practices, whereas attempts to reform the public sector in Syria, such as 'management by objectives' and Law No. 20 of 1994, have scarcely been implemented. As a result, while the public sector contributed positively to output and investment in Asian countries, the Syrian public sector did not.

Figure 5.4 Syria's Exports by International Blocks (1989-1999)
(% of Total Exports)

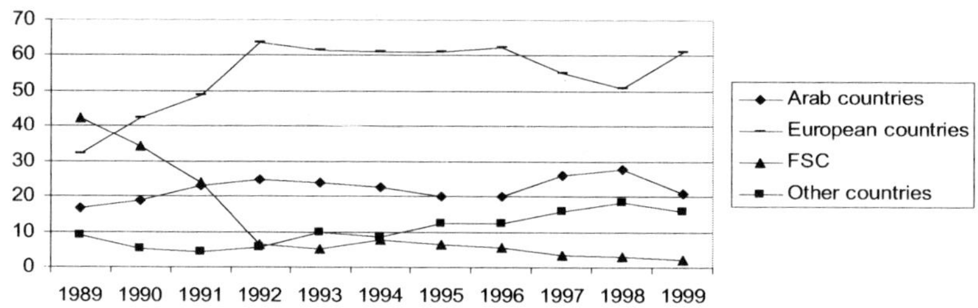

Source: Jooni (2001)

Finally, both China and Vietnam underwent significant structural transformation with an increase in the share of industry and services in their GDP. On the other hand, Syria scarcely witnessed any structural change during the nineties with only a slight increase in the share of rent seeking activities such as mining and agriculture. However, a similarity that can be drawn between the two experiences is that the limited financial liberalization in Asian countries, and its absence in Syria, have limited the SMEs access to credit and, therefore, hampered their growth and made them unable to create enough jobs and, in turn, exacerbated the unemployment and poverty problem. On the other hand, the performance of the Syrian economy in the 90s is similar, in many ways, to that of other resource abundant transition economies such as Uzbekistan. With the exports of natural resources maintaining the balance of payments, both countries implemented import substitution strategies, protected their domestic markets, achieved rapid recovery and delayed reforms, especially in financial and foreign trade liberalization. As a result, the growth collapse predicted for Uzbekistan (Auty 1999) was actually materialised in Syria.

On the whole, however, Syria's GDP path during transition (1986 - 1999) was quite positive in comparison with other transition countries, highly superior to both the averages of FSU and CEE countries and slightly lower than the path of Vietnam. Even when comparing with countries with the lowest cumulative output decline such as Poland, Slovak and Slovenia, Syria's GDP path was also considerably better.

Figure 5.5 GDP Path in Transition Time (pre-transition year = 100)

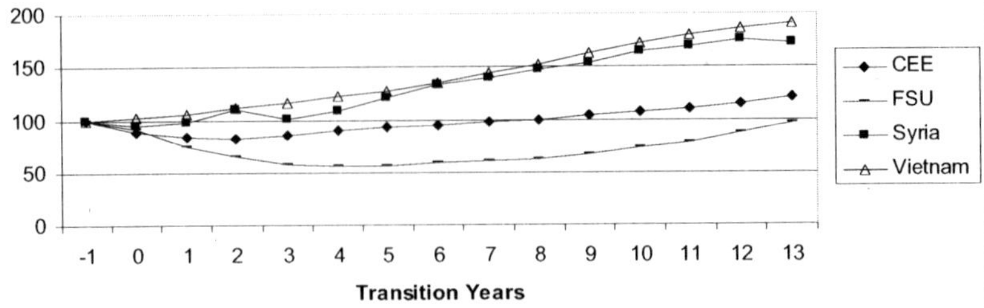

Source: Calculated from International Monetary Fund, World Economic Outlook Database, April 2008

Figure 5.6 GDP Path of Transition Countries with Lowest Cumulative Output Decline

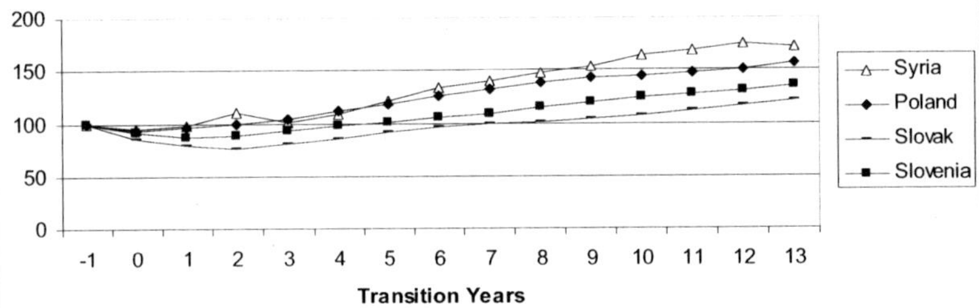

Source: Calculated from International Monetary Fund, World Economic Outlook Database, April 2008

2000-present: The Resumption of Reform

Reform Policy

Although it is too early to determine the final outcome of current reform as the process is still ongoing, it is still possible to sketch out their impact. By the beginning of the millennium, Syria was haunted by the mid-term outlook of declining oil prices anticipating the threat of an upcoming fiscal and balance of payments shocks. Consequently, Syria was facing two challenges: 1) achieving fiscal sustainability, and 2) diversifying the production and export base (International Monetary Fund 2005a, pp. 4). And just as the oil boom and high growth rates in the early 90s diminished the urgency of reform, the depleting oil reserves and the low growth rates in the late 90s encouraged the resumption of economic reform.

The year 2000 witnessed the announcement of economic reforms; however, these reforms lacked a clear strategy (Economic Research Forum 2006, pp. 35). Decree No.7 of 2000 and the amendment of Law No. 10 of 1991, could be viewed as incorporating the legal property rights (the rule of law) dimension to the investment climate.[10] The year 2001 witnessed the deregulation of the long time blocked real estate market by canceling old fixed rent contracts and sharing the value between owner and tenants. Most importantly, financial reform was initiated in the early 2000s by creating the necessary regulatory and supervisory framework for financial liberalization through setting up a Credit and Monetary Council with the task of designing monetary policy and regulating the licensing and registration procedures of banks and the confidentiality of the profession. And in 2004, private banks began to operate.

In the second half of the decade, private insurance companies, Islamic banks and foreign exchange bureaus and companies were allowed to operate. Moreover, the second half of the decade witnessed the creation of the Securities and Financial Markets authorities (Law No 22 of 2005) with the task of launching a stock exchange. The Damascus Securities Exchange (DSE) was established in 2006 (Decree No 55 of 2006) but was still has not operating in the spring of 2008.

As achieving fiscal sustainability became of major concern with depleting oil reserves, it was necessary to seek adjustments on both the revenue and the expenditure side of the budget. On the revenue side, a new Income Tax Law (Law No. 24) was passed in 2003 aiming at reducing tax evasion through lowering tax brackets and imposing severe penalties on tax evaders (Law for Combating Tax Evasion: Law No. 25) while widening the tax base by bringing in new activities not previously taxed. Moreover, a general consumption tax law was passed in 2004 replacing a large number of indirect taxes and acting as a transitional step before the adoption of VAT, representing a shift in Syria's tax policy towards indirect taxes. On the expenditure side, the Government pursued a policy of gradual reduction in subsidies which is most evident in the substantial decrease in the expenditure of the Price Stabilization Fund throughout the period (2000-2005) from 3.7% to 2% of GDP. Furthermore, there have been increases in the prices of petroleum products (diesel and gasoline)

Foreign trade and the exchange rate experienced considerable liberalization measures too. The maximum tariff rate has been lowered from 255 to 65% (IMF 2006, pp. 37) while the average tariff rate has been lowered from 20 percent in 2003 to 14.5 % in 2006 (IMF 2007, pp. 22). Important steps have been taken towards removing quantitative restrictions through tariffication, while positive lists of importable goods have been replaced with a negative list. And with the number of official exchange rates being reduced and their level adjusted, there has been a steady progress toward exchange rate unification. Moreover, Syria embarked on signing free trade agreements, most notably was GAFTA coming into force.

There has been a shift in fiscal policy from deflationary to expansionary, with an increase in the size of the government in order to compensate for the private sector's drawing back from investment during the second half of the 90s. This shift in fiscal policy represents a breakaway from budgetary discipline towards adopting a counter cyclical Keynesian policy. And for the first time since 1981, interest rates were lowered in 2003 and credit policy was eased by raising the ceiling on single loans and relaxing the collateral requirements.

The current wave of reforms has been much more comprehensive in comparison with the reforms undertaken in 1986-1991. And while the reforms of 1986-1991 had a much more tentative nature and were much more concerned with resolving the crisis in the economy through reducing public expenditure and seeking a private sector alternative, current reforms have shown a clear trend of shifting towards a market economy especially with the adoption of the social market economy in the 10th Five Year Plan. On the other hand, both waves of reforms have been selective. And while the reforms of 1986-1991 where confined to increasing openess to the private sector and price liberalization, the current wave of reforms has added trade and financial liberaization to its agenda. However, neither substantially targeted the reconstructing and privatization of the public sector or the broader issues of institutional reform.

Performance

The period 2000-2002 can be viewed as a continuation of the same framework that explains performance in the 90s. As in the late 90s, Syria's economy was influenced by the combination of a deflationary fiscal policy, overvalued real interest rates, and the absence of a second wave of reforms. Additionally, oil reserves were depleting and oil exports were declining and it was too early for contemporary reforms to have a significant positive effect on growth. Thus, Syria, at the outset of the new millennium, was trapped in a low growth situation. However, this low growth situation was cushioned by two external factors: a good harvest in 2001 and 2002, and a special trade agreement (2002-2003) with Iraq before the invasion, "similar to the one made with the former Soviet Union in 1989-1990, before its collapse" (Economic Research Forum 2006, pp. 35). This resulted in reasonable growth rates of (3.6%, 4.1%), and high non-oil growth rates of (7.6%, 7.5%) for the years 2001, 2002 respectively (Table 6.1).

Table 6.1 GDP Growth Rates 2000-2003

	2000	2001	2002	2003
Real GDP growth rate	0.6	3.6	4.1	1.1
Real non-oil GDP growth rate	1.6	7.6	7.5	2.5

Source: International Monetary Fund (2005b)

The year 2003 was gloomy with all external factors - declining oil exports, a bad harvest and regional conflict (the invasion of Iraq) – being negative and contributing to an economic slowdown. However, the expansionary fiscal and monetary policies adopted had the effect of cushioning the negative impacts of the above mentioned external factors (International Monetary Fund 2005a, pp. 10) and the year 2003 had a modest growth rate of 1.1%.

From 2004 onwards, Syria recovered benefiting from private exports and private investment due to excess liquidity in the Gulf Region, the implementation of GAFTA, increase in aggregate demand - due to the influx of Iraqi refugees - and an improved business climate (International Monetary Fund 2006, International Monetary Fund 2007). Moreover, the real estate boom associated with the influx of Iraqi refugees and its associated wealth effect, in addition to credit growth, public wage increases and good harvests all contributed to boosting consumption, and growth rates, albeit at the cost of increasing inflation and fiscal deficit (Table 6.2). By 2005, Syria's gross fixed capital formation began to restore its early 90s levels reaching approximately 25% of GDP (figure 6.1). While prior to 2004 the public sector was the main contributor to investment growth, from 2004 onwards the private sector increased its investment rates, exceeding that of the public sector.

Table 6.2 GDP Growth Rates 2004-2007				
	2004	2005	2006	2007
Real GDP growth rate	2.8	3.3	4.4	3.9
Real non-oil GDP growth rate	5	6	6.5	5.8

Source: International Monetary Fund (2007)

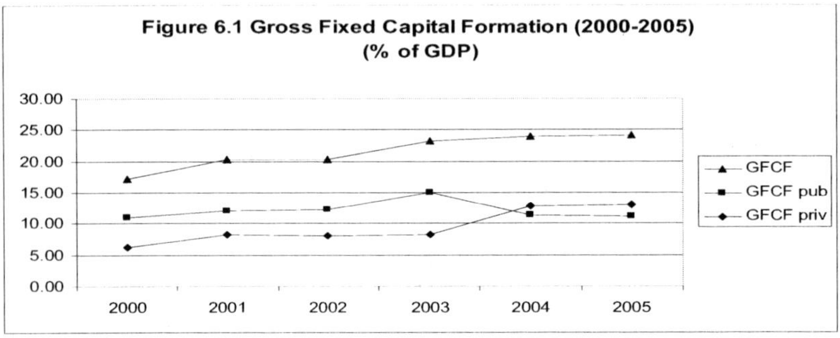

Source: Central Bureau of Statistics (2007)

With a decrease in oil exports and an increase in manufacturing exports (figure 6.3), trade has been gradually shifting from European countries to Arab countries; although it is still early to tell whether the increase in exports to Arab countries is a sustainable trend or just a temporary phenomenon (figure 6.2).

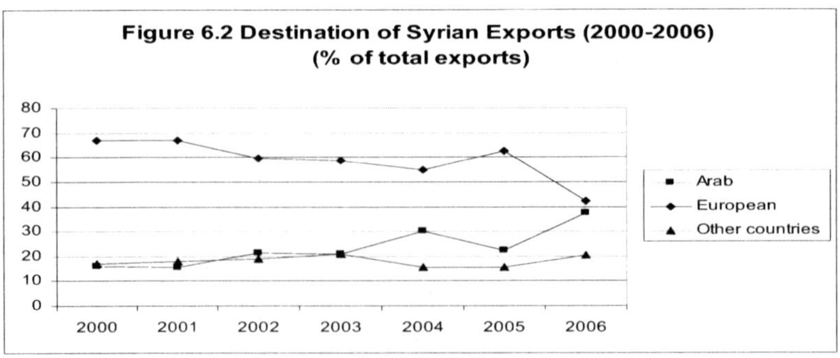

Source: Central Bureau of Statistics, Various Editions

Figure 6.3 Distribution of Exports by Economic Activity (2000-2006) (% of total exports)

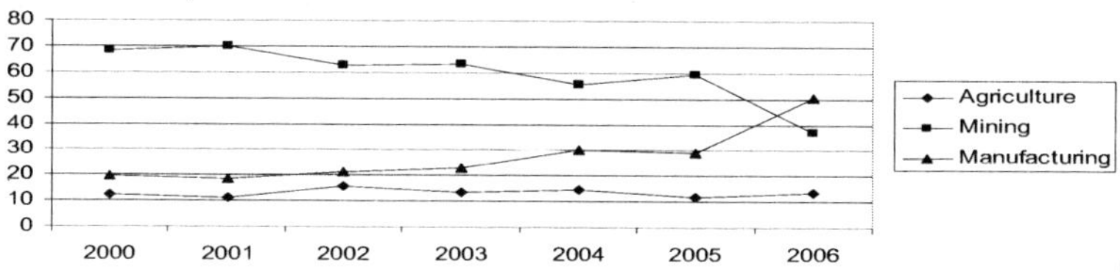

Source: Central Bureau of Statistics Various Editions

Figure 6.4 Credit to Public and Private Sectors (2000-2005) (% of GDP)

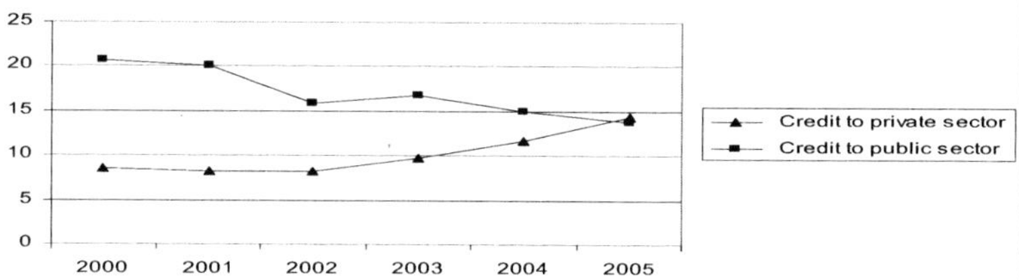

Source: International Monetary Fund (2005b and 2007

Furthermore, there have been positive signs regarding financial intermediation with the increase in private sector's access to credit surpassing the level of the public sector in 2005 (figure 6.4), and a slight increase in the share of credit allocated to industry and construction (Table 6.3).

Table 6.3 Allocation of Credit to Different Sectors (2000-2005)

	Agriculture	Wholesale and Distribu-tion	Industry and Mining	Construction	Services	Misc.
2000	10	72	2	9	1	6
2001	18	62	3	10	0	7
2002	25	51	4	12	0	8
2003	29	44	7	12	0	9
2004	24	41	8	15	0	12
2005	19	39	7	15	0	19

Source: Central Bureau of Statistics, Various Editions

Further Reform: Obstacles and Threats

Moving on with reform will be more difficult and the absence of reform in public administration threatens the effectiveness of the implementation of the reform process. The International Monetary Fund (2007) argues that the lack of technical expertise will make it hard to effectively implement legislation adopted in recent years. Moreover, weaknesses in data will impede the ability to monitor the impact of reforms and the capability of conducting macroeconomic management. While the absence of restructuring public enterprises will continue "to drain resources and hinder the growth of the private sector" (International Monetary Fund 2005a, pp. 8) The slow progress in state banks' restructuring - which are undercapitalized and suffer from high non-performing loans and low profitability – may entice these banks to obstruct further reforms in the banking sector thwarting the development of the competitiveness of the sector (International Monetary Fund 2007, pp. 21-22). Furthermore, there are many weaknesses in the regulatory and supervisory capacity of the banking sector, with the limited capability of evaluating the adequacy of banks' internal controls and their risk management practices. This is alarming in view of the recent credit expansion by private banks (International Monetary Fund 2007, pp. 22).

Overall, there is a need for restructuring the Central Bank so that it becomes an independent Central Bank with full supervisory authority over all banking institutions, declares price stability as the main objective of monetary policy, and develops monetary instruments for conducting monetary policy (e.g. liberalizing interest rates, issuing treasury bonds) and thus clearing the room for fiscal policy to influence aggregate demand.

Moving to the issue of fiscal sustainability and the need for adjustment on both sides of the budget, on the revenue side it is noted that although the ending of all tax exemptions offered under investment Law No. 10 of 1991 (Decree No 8 of 2007) can be viewed as an attempt towards broadening the tax base and rationalizing tax exemption, administrative capacity is still weak in mitigating tax evasion and implementing a comprehensive VAT. From the expenditure side, past oil revenues increased the amount of waste and decreased the effectiveness in both current and development expenditure; at present, neither expenditures are prioritized, nor are projects included in the budget preceded by feasibility studies (Economic Research Forum 2006, pp. 29). In view of the flaws on both sides of the budget, the mid-term aspect of the fiscal stance is quite worrisome. In particular, it questions the practicality of creating a 'social market economy' as mentioned in the 10th FYP through allocating additional resources to creating safety nets and tackling unemployment.

Figure 6.4 The Cost of Doing Business,Transition Countries

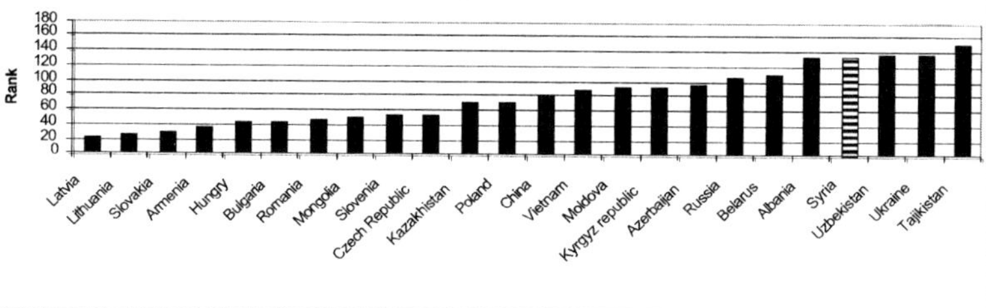

Source: Doing Business 2008, Various Country Reports

Finally, implementing institutional reforms aiming at strengthening competition, good governance, property rights, and the rule of law has been quite sluggish, and consequently, the cost of doing business has been high. According to the World Bank Group Doing Business Project index (figure 6.4), Syria is ranked 137 out of 178 countries and is among the highest in comparison with other transition countries along with other slow reformers (Uzbekistan, Ukraine, Belarus etc...). The absence of institutional reforms may induce the creation of oligopolies amid the liberalization of the economy.

Conclusion

Despite the structural differences between Syria and other transition countries as evident in the analysis of its initial conditions, Syria's economic performance can still be explained quite well by using an analytical framework of a transition economy. Syria's initial conditions, characterized by a low level of development and moderately high macroeconomic distortions, explain quite well its adoption of a gradual transition path. And although its level of macroeconomic distortions would have predicted a more severe initial output decline, the boom in oil exports, the assistance of the Soviet bloc and Syria's high market memory helped to mitigate these adverse shocks. The result was an output path akin to a shallow W shape curve holding a middle ground between the conventional U shape curve of CEE and FSU countries and the continuous high growth rates of Asian countries. Moreover, Syria's initial structural change comes in contrast with the experience of other transition countries with a fall in the share of its services sector instead of its industry sector reflecting the special characteristics of Syria's central planning years as a rentier state overdeveloped in comparison with its poor productive base.

Syria's transition experience is similar to the Asian transition countries of Vietnam and China in adopting a gradual dual track approach. However, Vietnam and China have been more successful in decentralising political power, revitalizating the public sector and aligning their economies with the global market. The boom in Syria's oil exports has diminished the inventives of taking such measures. This is a situation quite similar to the experience of other resource abundant transition economies where recovery was fast, reforms were delayed and the economy locked in a staple trap.

With oil exports declining and a fiscal and balance of payments crisis being anticipated, Syria has unleashed another wave of reforms. So far, Syria's growth rates are satisfactory and its fiscal and balance of payments deficits are still at manageable levels owing to the increase in oil prices and the increase in trade with Arab countries. However, the future is less certain, especially as low administrative capacity may hinder the successful implementation of further reforms. Moreover, the absence of broader institutional reforms may result in a non-competitive market economy with burgeoning oligarchies as the experience of "Former Soviet Union Countries" suggests.

---

[1] Staple trap refers to the outcome of a policy of transferring resource rents from potentially efficient sectors to less efficient activities, and thus leading to sustaining output in the short and medium run at the expense of adverse consequences in the long run.

[2] The transitory shock refers to the initial decline in the output of transition countries which is considered a necessary outcome of the introduction of hard budget constraints and the shift from a seller's to a buyer's market.

[3] The liberalization index (LI) was constructed originally by de Melo et al (1996). The index ranges from 0 to 1, and is calculated annually for each country based on a weighted average of three components: 1) Liberalizing internal markets (LII) (30%)--price liberalization, de-monopolization; 2) Liberalizing external markets (LIE) (30%)--reducing quantitative restrictions and tariffs; 3) Facilitating private sector entry (LIP) (40%)--privatization, private sector share, financial sector liberalization.

[4] The main difference between the de Melo et al (1997) transition model and other transition models lies in that the former includes a more comprehensive set of initial conditions in its analysis and extends the set of the

transition countries to include Vietnam and China. Another important aspect is that inflation, a measure of stabilization, is used – along with GDP growth – as the dependent variable, whereas inflation is usually the explanatory variable.

[5] It is acknowledged that the valuation of output represents a major measurement problem for all transition countries. However, most transition studies content themselves with official GDP figures due to the difficulty of finding consistent estimates of unofficial economy for the sample of countries over an extended period, (Havrylyshyn 2001, pp. 75). This study, in line with other transition studies will also rely on official data, while acknowledging that this will negatively affect the robustness of the conclusions drawn.

[6] The initial year of transition is different among different countries. For CEE, Mongolia and the FSU the initial year corresponds with the political changes that occurred in 1989-90 and 1991 respectively. Whereas for China, the initial year is defined with the shift to a more market-oriented economic policy in 1978; while 1986 is the initial year for both Vietnam and Syria corresponding with Vietnam's launching of the 'doi moi' reform program and Syria's foreign exchange crisis.

[7] de Melo et al (1997) rely on the 'repressed inflation' indicator. However, this indicator was not used for measuring macro distortions due to the difficulty in estimating repressed inflation in the early eighties in Syria. However, it is safe to assume that Syria was suffering from serious macroeconomic imbalances.

[8] 'Fictive exports' or 'fantasy exportation' refers to products that are exported across the border but not necessarily marketed abroad with the aim of obtaining an export document from Syrian customs in order to prove legal access to foreign exchange (Perthes 1992, pp. 47).

[9] The category 'Wholesale and Distribution' comprises mainly credit allocated for the procurement of cotton and wheat and other agricultural products

[10] The new decree established stronger legal protection for investors such as giving them the right of appeal before the Arab Investment Court or any other international jurisdiction arising from agreements signed between Syria and the country of the investor, and offering assurance to private investment that private assets cannot be expropriated or nationalized (Abu-Ismail et al 2002, pp. 84).

References

Abdel Nour, Ayman. (2001). "Syrian Views of an Association Agreement with the European Union." *EuroMeSCo Papers*, no. 14, pp. 1-19.

Abu-Ismail, Khalid, Ahmad Moustafa, and Matias Vernengo (2002). 'Trade and Industry' in UNDP Macroeconomic Policies for Poverty Reduction: The Case of Syria.

Abu-Ismail, Khalid. (2004). "The Syrian Economic Challenge," *Macroeconomic Policies for Poverty Reduction: The Case of Syria*. Damascus: UNDP, pp. 1-43.

Aita, Samir and Samir Seifan (2005). *Country Profile Syria*, Financial Chapter.

Albaladejo, Manuel and Sanjaya Lall (2004). "The Decline of Syrian Industry: An Assessment of Performance and Capabilities during the 1990s" Oxford Working Paper No.119

Amable, Bruno (2003). *The Diversity of Capitalism*, Oxford: Oxford University Press.

al-Amadi, Mohammed (2003). *Syria and the Process of Economic Integration* (in Arabic). Damascus: Syrian Economic Society.

Arkadie, V. Brian and Raymond Mallon (2003): "Viet Nam: A Transition Tiger?" Canberra: Asia Pacific Press at the Australia National University

Auty, R.M (1999): "Reforming Resource-Abundant Transition Economies: Kazakhstan and Uzbekistan," *IMF Working Paper* 9913

Berend, Ivan. T. (1995). Alternatives of transformation: choices and determinants -- East-Central Europe in the 1990s. *Markets, States, and Democracy: the Political Economy of Post-Communist Transformation*, in B. Crawford. Boulder, CO: Westview Press, pp. 130-149.

Biesbrouck, Wouter and Marvin Jackson (1995). "Markets and business competition: the institutional and economic framework." *Marketization, Restructuring and Competition in Transition Industries of Central and Eastern Europe*, in W. M. J. Biesbrouck. Aldershot: Avebury, pp. 31-91.

Brownlee, Jason. (2005). Political Crisis and Restabilization: Iraq, Libya, Syria and Tunisia. *Authoritarianism in the Middle East: Regimes and Resistance*. M. a. M. P. A. Prisptein Posusney. London, Lynne Rienner Publishers: 43-62.

Central Bureau of Statistics. (1983-2007) *Statistical Abstract*. Damascus: Syrian Arab Republic, Office of the Prime Minister, Series.

Compos, Nauro F. and Fabrizio Coricelli (2002): "Growth in Transition: What We Know, What We Don't, and What We Should" *Journal of Economic Literature* Vol. XL, September, pp.793-836

De Melo, Martha. Cevdet Denizer and Alan Gelb (1996): "From Plan to Market: Patterns of Transition," *World Bank Economic Review*, 10 (3), pp. 397-424.

De Melo, Martha, Cevdet Denzier, Alan Gelb, and Stoyan Tenev (1997): "Circumstance and Choice: The Role of Initial Conditions and Policies in Transition Economies", *World Bank Policy Research Working Paper No. 1866*, Washington: the World Bank.

Doing Business Project, World Bank Group (2008): "Doing Business 2008, Various Country Reports"

Economic Research Forum (2006): "Syria Country Profile: The Road Ahead for Syria, " February

Fischer, Stanley and Ratna Sahay (2000): "The Transition Economies after Ten Years," *NBER Working Paper* 7664

Hall, Peter A. and David Soskice. (2001) *Varieties of Capitalism*, Oxford: Oxford University Press.

Haverlysyn, Oleh (2001): "Recovery and Growth in Transition: A Decade of Evidence'' *IMF Staff Papers*, Vol.48, Special Issue pp. 53-87

Haverlysyn, Oleh and Ron van Rooden (2000): "Institutions Matter in Transition, But So Do Policies," *IMF Working Paper* 00/70

Heydemann, Steven. (1992). "The Political Logic of Economic Rationality: Selective Stabilization in Syria," in *The Politics of Economic Stabilization Programs in the Middle East*, ed. H. J. Barkey. New York: St. Martin's Press.

Hinnebusch, Raymond A. (1995) "The Political Economy of Economic Liberalization in Syria," *International Journal of Middle East Studies*,. 27 (3), pp. 305-320.

Horani, A. (2004). *The Effects of Interest Rate Change in the Context of Economic Reform* (In Arabic). Damascus: Syrian Economic Society.

al-Hussein, Muhammed. (July 6th, 2004). *Tax Reform: Its Aims and Scope* (in Arabic). Syrian Economic Society, Damascus, Syria.

International Monetary Fund (2005a): "Syrian Arab Republic: Staff Report for the 2005 Article IV Consultation," Country Report No. 05/356 October

----. (2005b): "Syrian Arab Republic: Statistical App.endix" Country Report No. 05/355, October

----. (2006): "Syrian Arab Republic: Staff Report for the 2006 Article IV Consultation," Country Report No. 06/294, August

----. (2007): "Syrian Arab Republic: Staff Report for the 2007 Article IV Consultation" Country Report No. 07/288, August

Jamil, Kadri (2001). *Prices and Wages: Elimination of Deficiency Between Prices and Wages...A Necessity for Economic Reform* (in Arabic), Damasucs: Syrian Economic Society.

Jamil, Kadri (June 1st, 2004). *The Reality of Economic Development and the Distribution of National Income* (in Arabic), Damascus: Syrian Economic Society.

Jooni, Ezzedin (2001): "El-Tijara El-Kharijiyeh El-Souriyeh" (Syrian Foreign Trade), Reda Publishing Press

Kanaan, Ali (2002): "El-Rokood Fee Souriyeh" (Stagnation in Syria), Damascus: Syrian Economic Society

al-Khatib, F. (2001). *Prices and Wages* (in Arabic), Damasucs: Syrian Economic Society.

Khoury, Issam (2002). "Free Trade Zones as a motivation for Economic Reforms and a `Booster for inter-Arab State Trade" (in Arabic), Damascus: Syrian Economic Society..

Kolodko, Grzegorz. W. (1999). "Transition to a market economy and sustained growth. Implications for the post-Washington consensus," *Communist and Post-Communist Studies*, 32, pp. 233-261.

Kornai, Janos. (1992). *The Socialist System: The Political Economy of Communism*. Oxford: Clarendon Press.

Kumssa, Asfaw and John F. Jones (1999). "The social consequences of reform in transitional economies." *International Journal of Social Economics*, 26 (1/2/3), pp. 194-210.

Lane, David (2005). "Social Class as a Factor in the Transformation of State Socialism," *Journal of Communist Studies and Transition Politics*, 21 (4), pp. 417-435.

Lau, Lawrence, Yingyi Qian and Gérard Roland (1997). "Pareto-Improving Economic Reforms through Dual-Track Liberalization." *Economic Letters,* 55(2), pp. 285-292.

Lau, Lawrence, Yingyi Qian and Gérard Roland (2000). "Reform Without Losers: An Interpretation of China's Dual-Track Approach." *Journal of Political Economy,* 108 (1), pp. 120-143.

Mizobata, Satoshi (2007). "The Consequences of the Transformation on the Third World," in Lane, David (ed.). *The Transformation of State Socialism: System Change, Capitalism or Something Else?*, Palgrave, New York, pp. 286-300.

Nejmeh, Elias (September 23rd, 2003). *Syrian Financial Policy* (in Arabic), Damascus: Syrian Economic Society.

Papava, Vladamir. (2005). "On the theory of post-Communist economic transition to market." *International Journal of Social Economics*, 32, (1/2), pp. 77-97.

Perthes, Volker (1992): "The Syrian Economy in the 1980s," *Middle East Journal,* 46 (1). pp. 37-58

----. (2001). "The Political Economy of Syrian Sucession." *Survival*, 43(1), pp. 143-54.

Polling, Sylvia. (1998). "Overall Economic Developments and Reform Policies" in *Scenarios for Syria: Socio-Economic and Political Choices*, Volker. Perthes (ed.). Baden-Baden, Nomos Verlagsgesellschaft: 41-58.

Rodrick, Dani and Arvind Subramanian (2003). "The primacy of institutions." *Finance and Development*, pp. 31-34.

Roland, Gerard and Thierry Verdier (1999). "Transition and output fall." *Economics of Transition*, 7(1): 1-28.

Sader, Makram (2001). *The Modernization of the Syrian Banking System* (in Arabic). Damasucs: Syrian Economic Society.

Seifan, Samir. (March 13th, 2001). *Tax avoidance and smuggling...a frank approach* (in Arabic), Damascus: Syrian Economic Society.

Shahlawi, Kosti. (2001). *Modernizing the Banking System* (in Arabic). Damascus: Syrian Economic Society.

Shallah, Ratib (2001). *Banking System Reforms* (in Arabic), Damascus: Syrian Economic Society.

Shevchenko, Alexei (2004). "Bringing the party back in: the CCP and the trajectory of market transition in China." *Communist and Post-Communist Studies*, 37(2): 161-85.

State Planning Commission., SAR (2006a). *The Framework for Financial Sector Reform in Syria*, Damascus.

----. (2006b). *Highlights of the Syrian Economy and the Tenth 5YP Strategy,* Damascus: State Planning Commission.

----. (2006b). *The Management of Economic Planning in Syria*, Damascus: State Planning Commission.

Sukkar, Nabil. (2000). *Economic Reform in Syria* (in Arabic). Beirut, Riy'ad al-Rayyis lil-Kutub wa-al-Nashr.

----. (May 25th, 2004). *The Banking System in Syria, between Reform and Opening* (in Arabic). Damascus: Syrian Economic Society.

Suleiman, Adnan (2005). *Status and Perspectives of Investment in Syrian Free Zones* (in Arabic), Damascus: Syrian Economic Society.

Sutela, Pekka (1992). "The role of the external sector during the transition," in *The Post-Soviet Economy: Soviet and Western Perspectives*, ed. A. Aslund. New York, St. Martin's Press, pp. 85-101.

Tisdell, Clem (2001). "Transitional economies and economic globalisation: Social and environmental consequences." *International Journal of Social Economics*, 28 (5/6/7), pp. 577-590.

Van Arkadie Brian, and Do Duc Dinh (2004), "Economic Reform in Tanzania and Vietnam: A Comparative Commentary," William Davidson Institute Working Paper Number 706, June

Wedeman, Andrew Hall (2003). *From Mao to Market: rent seeking, local protectionism and marketization in China*. Cambridge: Cambridge University Press.

Wilson, Jeanne (2007). "China's Transformation towards Capitalism," in Lane, David and Marin Myant (eds.). *Varieties of Capitalism in Post-Communist Countries*, Palgrave, New York, pp. 239-257.

Wu, Fulong (2004). "Urban poverty and marginalization under market transition: the case of Chinese cities." *International Journal of Urban and Regional Research* 28, (2), pp. 401-423.

Yarbrough, Beth V., Robert M. Yarbrough (1997). *The World Economy: Trade and Finance.* Fort Worth, TX: The Dryden Press.

Ye, Meng-Hua (1991). "The Privatization of State-Owned Enterprises in Eastern European Countries." *Papers of the Center for Modern China*, 14.

al-Zaim, Isam. (February 27, 2001). *The Background of Economic Reform in Syria* (Arabic), Damascus: Syrian Economic Society.

About the Authors

Samer Abboud is assistant professor of political science at Susquehanna College.

Ferdinand Arslanian is an economist and project consultant with the German Technical Cooperation Agency in Damascus.

The St Andrews Papers on Modern Syrian Studies is published by the Centre for Syrian Studies, University of St Andrews, Scotland and distributed by Lynne Rienner Publishers, Boulder, CO, USA. The series remit is to publish cutting edge contemporary research and analysis on modern Syria, with the focus on the contemporary economic "transition" (reform) and on Syria's current security problems.
http://www.st-andrews.ac.uk/~wwwir/syrian/

We invite submission of unsolicited papers, particularly papers that report on current empirical research on Syria. Send paper submissions to series editor, Raymond Hinnebusch, School of International Relations, University of St Andrews, St Andrews, Fife, Scotland, KY15 7SP, U.K. or by e-mail to rh10@st-andrews.ac.uk.